Rails-to-Trails

FLORIDA

"There's no better guide for these multipurpose trails. Like the Rails-to-Trails system, this series is a service that's long overdue."

—Sarah Parsons, Associate Editor, *Sports Afield*

"Recreation trails are one of America's great outdoor secrets, but probably won't be for much longer thanks to the Rails-to-Trails Conservancy Guidebook Series. Now adventurers of all abilities have an excellent guide to help them enjoy all that the paths have to offer."

—Stephen Madden, Editor-in-Chief, *Outdoor Explorer*

Help Us Keep This Guide Up to Date

Every effort has been made by the author and editors to make this guide as accurate and useful as possible. However, many things can change after a guide is published— trails are rerouted, establishments close, phone numbers change, facilities come under new management, and so on.

We would love to hear from you concerning your experiences with this guide and how you feel it could be improved and kept up to date. While we may not be able to respond to all comments and suggestions, we'll take them to heart and we'll also make certain to share them with the author. Please send your comments and suggestions to the following address:

The Globe Pequot Press
Reader Response/Editorial Department
P.O. Box 480
Guilford, CT 06437

Or you may e-mail us at:

editorial@globe-pequot.com

Thanks for your input, and happy travels!

Great Rail-Trails Series

THE OFFICIAL

Rails-to-Trails

CONSERVANCY GUIDEBOOK

Florida

by
David Gluckman

The Globe Pequot Press

SOUTH HOLIDAY
BRANCH

Guilford, Connecticut

Copyright © 2001 by The Globe Pequot Press

Cover illustration: Neal Aspinall
Cover design: Nancy Freeborn
Text design: Lesley Weissman-Cook
Maps: Tim Kissel/Trailhead Graphics, Inc., copyright © The Globe Pequot Press

Photo credits: David Gluckman

Library of Congress Cataloging-in-Publication Data
Gluckman, David
    Rails-to-Trails. Florida/David Gluckman. — 1st ed.
        p. cm. — (Great rail-trails series)
    Includes index.
    ISBN 0-7627-0712-7
        1. Rail-trails—Florida—Guidebooks. 2. Outdoor recreation—
    Florida   —Guidebooks. 3. Florida—Guidebooks. I. Title. II. Series.

GV191.42.F6 G58 2001
917.5409'64—dc21   00-064643

Manufactured in the United States of America
First Edition/Third Printing

CONTENTS

THE FLORIDA TRAIL SYSTEM 85

TOP STATE PARK TRAILS   94

ACKNOWLEDGMENTS

A special thanks to my wife, Casey, for editing the manuscript and keeping me company on the 5,000 miles of driving it took to gather data on the trails in this guide. Thanks to the employees of the Office of Greenways and Trails and the Florida Park Service in the Florida Department of Environmental Protection, as well as the great work of the staff of the Florida Field Office of the Rails-to-Trails Conservancy: Jeff Ciabotti, Heidi Holcolm, and the boss, Ken Bryan. Without your help, and that of lots of others in local parks and recreation departments around the state, this guide would not have been written. Thanks again to all of you.

INTRODUCTION

O ur pace is so fast. In the ever-changing and evolving world of technology, we literally cannot keep up with the times. Once upon a time the train seemed like the epitome of the modern world. Sleek and bold trains were our nation's pride and joy and symbolized the possibilities of a world beyond the one in which we lived. Connecting large cities and small towns, used for transportation and for the shipping of goods, the train was the pulse of the nation.

But times change. With the advent of the car and the building of mass highways, trains became a secondary form of transportation. And dreams die. Railroad tracks were abandoned. Nature took over and where once a track split through the woods, only a ghost of the track remained.

Enter the Rails-to-Trails Conservancy (RTC), a group of outdoor enthusiasts who in 1986 began the arduous task of transforming abandoned railroad tracks into nature trails. Banding together with other conservation groups, RTC removed tracks and molded the trails into wonderful paths running through urban and rural areas.

Rails-to-Trails

There is something remarkable about traveling the nation in pursuit of the abandoned railroad track now converted to greenways, bicycle paths, and nature trails. What better way to see the country than by traversing these rail beds?

Where once a dream was lost, it now is recovered with the advent of more and more rail-trails. So, hop on your bike or horse, put on a pair of hiking boots, or lace up those in-line skates. It's time to explore rail-trails!

The History of the Rails-to-Trails Conservancy

The beauty of RTC is that by converting railroad rights-of-way for public use, it has not only preserved a part of our nation's history but also allowed a variety of outdoor enthusiasts to enjoy the paths and trails.

Bicyclists, in-line skaters, nature lovers, hikers, equestrians, and paddlers can enjoy the trails, as can railroad history buffs. All of Florida's rail-trails are wheelchair accessible. Throughout Florida, there are thirty active RTC trails, and each year more are added. You can find trails near cities and rural trails far from the madding crowd. In many ways we have come full circle. By preserving part of our history, we can enjoy the trails as if time stood still.

The concept of preserving these valuable corridors and converting them into multiuse public trails began in the Midwest, where railroad abandonments were most widespread. Once the tracks came out, people started using the corridors for walking and hiking while exploring railroad relics ranging from train stations and mills to bridges and tunnels.

Although many people agreed with the great new concept, the reality of actually converting abandoned railroad corridors into public trails was a much greater challenge. From the late 1960s until the early 1980s, many rail-trail efforts failed as corridors were lost to development, sold to the highest bidder, or broken into pieces.

In 1983 Congress enacted an amendment to the National Trails System Act directing the Interstate Commerce Commission to allow about-to-be-abandoned railroad lines to be "railbanked," or set aside for future transportation use while being used as trails in the interim. In essence this law preempts rail corridor abandonment, keeping the corridors intact for trail use and any possible future use.

This powerful new piece of legislation made it easier for agencies and organizations to acquire rail corridors for trails, but many projects still failed because of short deadlines, lack of information, and local opposition to trails.

The Rails-to-Trails Conservancy was formed in 1986 to provide a national voice for the creation of rail trails. RTC quickly developed a strategy to preserve the largest amount of rail corridor in the shortest period of time: a national advocacy program to defend the new railbanking law in the courts and in Congress, coupled with a direct project-assistance program to help public agencies and local rail-trail groups overcome the challenges of converting a rail into a trail.

The strategy is working. In 1986 the Rails-to-Trails Conservancy knew of only seventy-five rail-trails and ninety projects in the works. Today there are more than 1,000 rail-trails, and many additional projects are under way. The RTC vision of creating an interconnected network of trails across the country is becoming a reality.

The thriving rails-to-trails movement has created more than 7,700 miles of public trails for a wide range of users. People across the country are now realizing the incredible benefits of rail-trails.

Benefits of Rail-Trails

Rail-trails are flat or have gentle grades, making them perfect for multiple users ranging from walkers and bicyclists to in-line skaters and people with disabilities.

In urban areas rail-trails act as linear greenways through developed areas, efficiently providing much-needed recreation space while serving as utilitarian transportation corridors. They link neighborhoods and workplaces and connect congested areas to open spaces. In many cities and suburbs, rail-trails are used for commuting to work, school, and shopping.

In rural areas rail-trails can provide a significant stimulus to local businesses. People who use trails often spend money on food, beverages, camping, hotels, bed-and-breakfasts, bicycle rentals, souvenirs, and other items. Studies have shown that trail users have generated as much as $1.25 million annually for a town through which a trail passes.

Rail-trails preserve historic structures, such as train stations, bridges, tunnels, mills, factories, and canals. These structures shel-

Biking in Oscar Sherer State Park

ter an important piece of history and enhance the trail experience.

Wildlife enthusiasts can enjoy the rail-trails, which are home to birds, plants, wetlands, and small and large mammals. Many rail-trails serve as plant and animal conservation corridors, and, in some cases, endangered species can be found in habitats located along the route.

Recreation, transportation, historic preservation, economic revitalization, open-space conservation, and wildlife preservation—these are just some of the many benefits of rail-trails and the reasons why people love them.

The strongest argument for the rail-to-trails movement, however, is ultimately about the human spirit. It's about the dedication of individuals who have a dream and follow that vision so that other people can enjoy the fruits of their labor.

How to Get Involved

If you really enjoy rail-trails, there are opportunities to join the movement to save abandoned rail corridors and to create more trails. Donating even a small amount of your time can help get more trails up and going. Here are some ways you can help the effort:

- Write a letter to your city, county, or state elected official in favor of pro-trail legislation. You can also write a letter to the editor of your local newspaper highlighting a trail or trail project.

- Attend a public hearing to voice support for a local trail.
- Volunteer to plant flowers or trees along an existing trail or spend several hours helping a cleanup crew on a nearby rail-trail project.
- Lead a hike along an abandoned corridor with your friends or a community group
- Become an active member on a trail effort in your area. Many groups host trail events, undertake fund-raising campaigns, publish brochures and newsletters, and carry out other activities to promote a trail or project. Virtually all of these efforts are completed by volunteers and they are always looking for another helping hand.

Whatever your time allows, get involved. The success of a community's rail-trail depends upon the level of citizen participation. The Rail-to-Trails Conservancy enjoys both local and national support. By joining RTC you will get discounts on all of its publications and merchandise while supporting the largest national trails organization in the United States. To become a member, use the order form at the back of the book.

How to Use Rail-Trails

By design, rail-trails accommodate a variety of trail users. While this is generally one of the many benefits of rail-trails, it also can lead to occasional conflicts among trail users. Everyone should take responsibility to ensure trail safety by following a few simple trail etiquette guidelines.

One of the most basic etiquette rules is "Wheels yield to heels." The figure below indicates the correct protocol for yielding right-of-way. Bicyclists (and in-line skaters) yield to other users; pedestrians yield to equestrians.

Generally, this means that you need to warn users (to whom you are yielding) of your presence. If, as a bicyclist, you fail to warn a walker that you are about to pass, the walker could step in front of you, causing an accident that could have been prevented. Similarly, it is best to slow down and warn an equestrian of your presence. A horse can be startled by a bicycle, so make verbal contact with the rider and be sure it is safe to pass.

Here are some other guidelines you should follow to promote trail safety:

- Obey all trail rules posted at trailheads.
- Stay to the right except when passing.
- Pass slower traffic on their left; yield to oncoming traffic when passing.
- Give a clear warning signal when passing.
- Always look ahead and behind when passing.
- Travel at a responsible speed.
- Keep pets on a leash.
- Do not trespass on private property.
- Move off the trail surface when stopped to allow others to pass.
- Yield to other trail users when entering and crossing the trail.
- Do not disturb the wildlife.
- Do not swim in areas not designated for swimming.
- Watch out for traffic when crossing the street.
- Obey all traffic signals.

How to Use This Book

Rails-to-Trails Florida is one of a series of state and regional trail guides produced by the Rails-to-Trails Conservancy in partnership with Globe Pequot Press that will ultimately describe all the rail-trails around the country. Though this guide also includes some interesting Florida state park trails, that is not its primary emphasis, nor will future books in this series necessarily include trails other than rail-trails.

Florida rail-trails have no sharp curves or steep inclines. Paved, they serve as multiuse recreational and alternative transportation facilities or linear parks. Unpaved, they are used as hiking, equestrian, or off-road bicycle trails.

Stopping at a trailhead

At the beginning of the book, you will find a map showing the location of Florida's rail-trails. The text description of every trail begins with the following information:

- **Name:** The official name of the rail-trail.
- **Activities:** A list of icons tells you what kinds of activities are appropriate for each trail.
- **Location:** The county or counties through which the trail passes.
- **Length:** The length of the trail, including how many miles are currently open and, for those trails that are built on partially abandoned corridors, the number of miles actually on the rail line.
- **Surface:** The materials that make up the rail-trail vary from trail to trail. This heading describes each trail's surface. Materials range from asphalt and crushed stone to the significantly more rugged original railroad ballast.
- **Wheelchair access:** All of Florida's rail-trails are wheelchair accessible. This allows physically challenged individuals the opportunity to explore the rail-trails with family and friends.
- **Difficulty:** Rail-trails range from easy to difficult, depending on the grade of the trail and its general condition. In Florida all rail-trails are easy.

- **Food:** Here we will indicate the towns and areas near the rail-trails in which restaurants and fast-food shops are available.
- **Rest room facilities:** If a rest room is available near the trail, the book will provide you with its location.
- **Seasons:** All of Florida's trails are open year-round.
- **Access and parking:** The book will provide you with locations where you can park to access the rail-trails. If public transportation is available to a town through which the trail passes, it will be noted here as well.
- **Rentals:** Some of the rail-trails have bicycle shops and skating stores nearby. This will help you with bike or skate rental information. If you are having problems with your equipment, you can have it checked out at the store.
- **Contact:** The name and contact information for each trail manager is listed here. The selected contacts are generally responsible for managing the trail and can provide additional information about the trail and its condition.
- **Map:** The main rail-trails and state park trails featured in this book include basic maps for your convenience. It's recommended, however, that street maps, topographic maps such as USGS quads, or a state atlas be used to supplement the maps in this book.
- **Mile-by-mile description:** The major rail-trails featured will have a mile-by-mile description allowing you the chance to anticipate the experience of the trail.

This book is intended as a user's guide to the best rail-trails and state park trails in Florida as well as an introduction to the future comprehensive state trail system. Because of the speed at which this system is expanding, the information here is bound to be out of date before to long. That's good! The state of Florida is growing at a rapid rate and changing all the time. We did not include more information on local fueling, sleeping, and eating accommodations because you can never be sure what you'll find next year or the year after. We did try to include a little history, because that's a lot harder to change. If you intend to rely on any of the information for your comfort and supply, please check with rail-trail managers before embarking. That's what the included phone numbers and addresses are there for.

Good luck with your travels and enjoy the ride!

Key to Activities Icons

Backpacking

Bird-watching

Camping

Dog Walking

Golf Cart Riding

Fishing

Historic Sites

Horseback Riding

In-line Skating

Mountain Biking

Paddlesports

Road Bicycling

Running

Swimming

Walking/Dayhiking

Wildlife Viewing

Key to Map Icons

P Parking

I Information

Rest Rooms

R Rentals

A Camping

Rails-to-Trails

FLORIDA

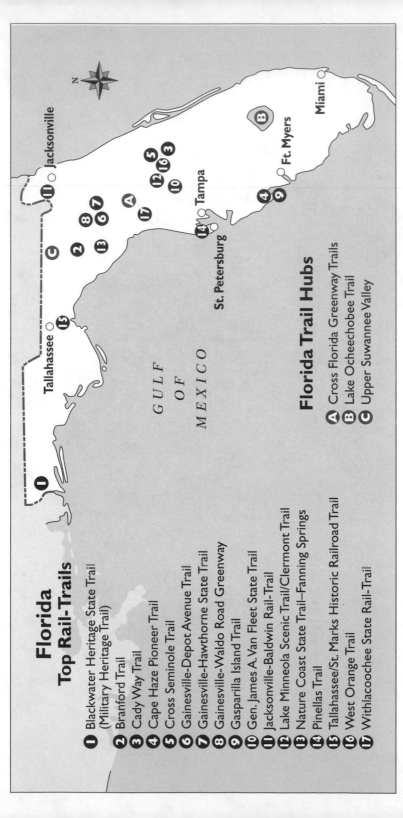

Florida
Top Rail-Trails

❶ Blackwater Heritage State Trail (Military Heritage Trail)
❷ Branford Trail
❸ Cady Way Trail
❹ Cape Haze Pioneer Trail
❺ Cross Seminole Trail
❻ Gainesville–Depot Avenue Trail
❼ Gainesville–Hawthorne State Trail
❽ Gainesville–Waldo Road Greenway
❾ Gasparilla Island Trail
❿ Gen. James A. Van Fleet State Trail
⓫ Jacksonville–Baldwin Rail-Trail
⓬ Lake Minneola Scenic Trail/Clermont Trail
⓭ Nature Coast State Trail–Fanning Springs
⓮ Pinellas Trail
⓯ Tallahassee/St. Marks Historic Railroad Trail
⓰ West Orange Trail
⓱ Withlacoochee State Rail-Trail

Florida Trail Hubs

Ⓐ Cross Florida Greenway Trails
Ⓑ Lake Ocheechobee Trail
Ⓒ Upper Suwannee Valley

GULF
OF
MEXICO

Jacksonville
Tallahassee
Tampa
St. Petersburg
Ft. Myers
Miami

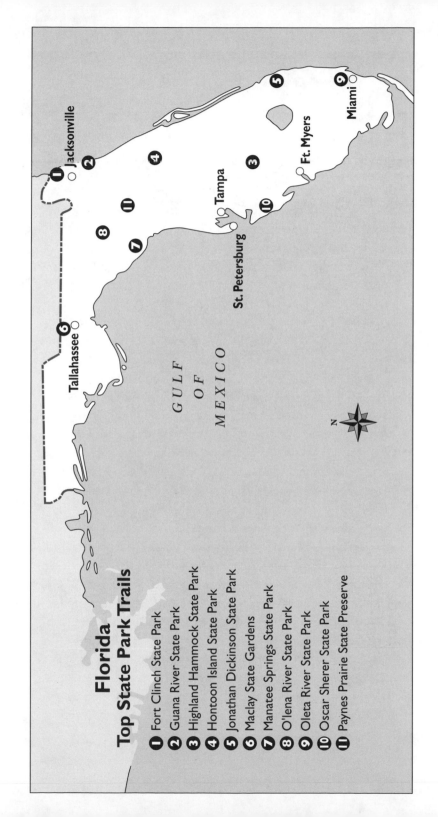

Florida
Top State Park Trails

1 Fort Clinch State Park
2 Guana River State Park
3 Highland Hammock State Park
4 Hontoon Island State Park
5 Jonathan Dickinson State Park
6 Maclay State Gardens
7 Manatee Springs State Park
8 O'lena River State Park
9 Oleta River State Park
10 Oscar Sherer State Park
11 Paynes Prairie State Preserve

Jacksonville

Tallahassee

Tampa

St. Petersburg

Ft. Myers

Miami

GULF
OF
MEXICO

N

BEFORE YOU START

Florida's trails teem with wildlife—some species to look for and others to look out for. Common critters that you'll enjoy seeing include mice, rabbits, squirrels, skunks, raccoons, opossums, and armadillos. Foxes, deer, and feral hogs are occasional sights, as are the elusive black bears. Gopher tortoises are surprisingly common on rail-trails. And the state features more than 500 bird species, including both year-round residents and a wide range of migratories.

Florida's snake population is generally pretty healthy, although loss of habitat and needless killing are taking their toll. Along with many nonpoisonous types, the state hosts all four of the poisonous snake groups found in the United States: ground (pygmy) and diamondback rattlesnakes; coral snakes; water moccasins; and copperheads (northern Florida only).

Once endangered, the state's alligator population is healthy and growing. These critters are rarely aggressive; if you do run into one on a trail, make a lot of noise and wait for it to move. If it's a small gator, you can just push it off with a stick. But don't make it mad: Surprisingly, it can run faster than you for the first 25 feet.

Florida's insect populations are vibrant indeed! Mosquitoes, yellow or deerflies, dog flies, no-see-ums, ticks, chiggers, and fire ants may all pose problems. Follow all the usual precautions and remember not to scratch.

Almost every unpaved shady spot in Florida will host a healthy crop of poison ivy at one time or another during the year. Watch where you rest your body. Thorny vegetation such as blackberry bushes, smilax vines, sandspurs, and prickly pear cacti may also pose a threat to your bicycle tires.

Florida weather can range from very hot to surprisingly cold, although the state is generally mild compared to the North. The best times of year for outdoor recreation are from late fall through the winter and into early spring. If you're on a summer outing, drink lots of fluids and save strenuous activities for early morning.

Rainfall averages 55 inches a year in the state, with almost half of that arriving during big storms or fronts. Summer rains or thunderstorms commonly arrive every afternoon. These storms can be severe, with lots of lightning; follow the usual precautions. Nobody has any business outdoors during a tornado or hurricane.

Florida's

TOP RAIL-TRAILS

Blackwater Heritage State Trail (Military Heritage Trail)

This is the westernmost rail-trail in the state, extending from the small community of Milton in the south to Whiting Field Naval Air Station (NAS) in the north. It's actually two trails, one managed by the Florida Park Service (Blackwater) and the other by the U.S. Navy (Military), but it's hard to tell where one leaves off and the other begins. It's mostly a rural trail, with only a few dwellings at some of the crossroads once you leave Milton and before you get on the military base. There are some nice creek crossings on wooden bridges with few hills or grades. This is a pleasant trip for the whole family with lots of access and safe travel.

Activities:

Location: Santa Rosa County

Length: Blackwater 7.0 miles; Military 2.2 miles; total 9.2 miles

Surface: Asphalt; 12 feet wide

Wheelchair access: Throughout its length

Difficulty: Easy

Food: You'll find every fast-food restaurant you'd want (and a few you wouldn't) in Milton along US 90 near the trailhead. The only other food source is the canteen on the NAS.

Rest room facilities: At the trailheads in Milton and the NAS.

Seasons: Open all year.

Access and parking: In addition to the corner of US 90 and County Road 87 just east of Milton (parking, rest rooms and water), you can access the trail from the Munson Highway Trailhead (parking only); the Whiting Field NAS

Trailhead at the outlying property boundary (parking only); and the NAS itself (public access permitted). The Greyhound Bus will get you to Milton, but the rest of the trip you'll be on your own. Check the bike shop across from the trailhead for other available transportation to the NAS.

Rentals: The Truly Spok'n bike shop at the trailhead in Milton has some rentals.

Contact: Blackwater River State Park, 7720 Deaton Bridge Road, Holt, FL 32564; (850) 983–5363.

• •

T his part of Florida is typified by rolling sandy hills and pine plantations interspersed with cypress bayheads, titi swamps, and some hardwood hammocks along the rivers. You can expect to see gopher tortoises, alligators, and white-topped pitcher plants in the wetlands if you look carefully. The Blackwater Heritage State Trail goes through all of these habitats as it leisurely travels from Milton in the south, with its municipal buildings clustered near the trail, to the high-tech airfield at the NAS in the north.

The trail was constructed on the raised bed of the former Florida and Alabama Railroad, which was in turn built in the early 1900s to transport lumber to the mill in Bagdad, a mile south of Milton. When the timber industry faltered in the late 1930s, the mill closed and the railroad ceased operation. When Whiting Field NAS was opened in 1942, the line was reopened, and a sample still exists in the West Florida Railroad Museum in Milton. The corridor was purchased by the state in 1993 and opened to the public as a paved rail-trail in 1998.

To reach it, take exit 8 (State Road 191) off I–10 through Bagdad into east Milton and turn left onto US 90. The Milton Trailhead is on the corner of US 90 and State Road 89. As you approach Milton from the east, turn right onto State Road 78 and directly right onto Elva Street just past the Tastee Freeze into the parking lot. The trailhead sign and facilities are visible from US 90.

The trail is elevated a few feet along most of its length and crosses small creeks on substantial wooden bridges. Horses are encouraged to use the unpaved portions of the rights-of-way and to cross creeks on the same bridges as the other users. There are no consistent mileage markers.

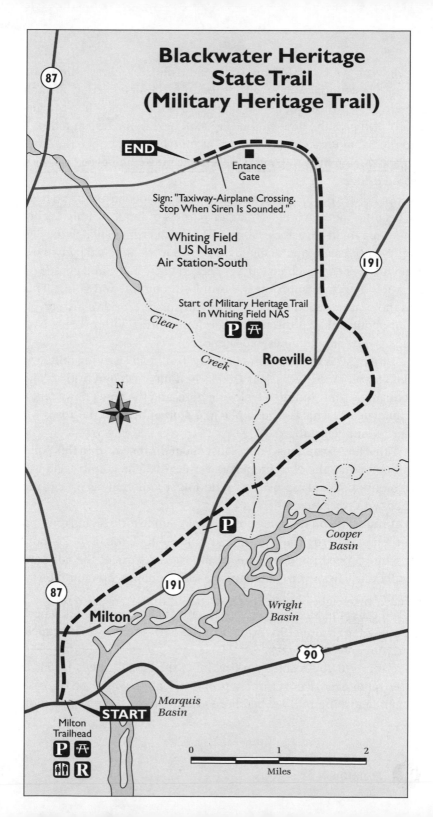

Blackwater Heritage State Trail (Military Heritage Trail)

87

END

■ Entance Gate

Sign: "Taxiway-Airplane Crossing. Stop When Siren Is Sounded."

Whiting Field US Naval Air Station-South

191

Start of Military Heritage Trail in Whiting Field NAS

P **⩫**

Clear *Creek*

Roeville

N

P

Cooper Basin

Wright Basin

87

191

Milton

90

Marquis Basin

START

Milton Trailhead

P **⩫**
⛹ **R**

0   1   2

Miles

Leaving from the Milton Trailhead, the trail's first mile leads through residential Milton with wooden fence-line barriers at each crossroad and nice wooden bridges across the creeks (five bridges in all). You pass the new Milton City Hall next to the trail at mile 0.7 and the Santa Rosa County Library at mile 0.9. The equestrian trail starts about 1.0 mile out and travels adjacent to the paved trail with shared bridges.

The houses begin to thin out at mile 1.3 as wooded areas and trailers become more evident on larger parcels of land. At mile 1.7 beware free-ranging livestock at one of the small farms. Though they've surely graced someone's table by now, we were attacked by two big male turkeys that gobbled loudly, pecked vigorously, and chased us for a few hundred yards on the trail both coming and going. This was the first recorded rail-trail turkey attack in Florida's history.

At about mile 2.0 the trail enters pine forest with cypress bayheads. A few small homesteads appear.

At mile 2.8 is the Munson Highway Trailhead (parking only). At mile 3.5 you cross over Clear Creek on a nice wooden bridge. The floodplain is a few hundred feet wide here, and the creek flows rapidly underneath. This is a good place to stop and smell the roses (or other swamp vegetation).

With a few exceptions, houses just about disappear from this point until you reach the NAS property at mile 7.0. The countryside is a combination of upland planted pine forest and cypress-titi swamp mixed with bay trees.

At mile 3.9 you can see some active gopher tortoise burrows on your left side of the trail. Starting at mile 4.0 look for 18- to 24-inch-tall white-topped pitcher plants in the wetter parts of the adjacent woodlands. These very active insect-eating plants are common in this area.

You cross the Munson Highway again at about 6.15 miles. There are a few farms along this stretch to the NAS property. The equestrian trail ends at mile 6.9.

At mile 7.0 you reach a parking lot at the NAS Trailhead. This is on the outer edge of government property, before you reach the base proper. Leave the railroad bed here and travel on a curving section

One of the bridges across a small creek running into the Blackwater River

through some landscaped areas with flower beds and small oaks into what looks like a wide mown parkway. The Munson Highway, which leads into the NAS, is on your left.

Along the parkway are nice benches every 0.25 mile made from recycled plastic attached to 4- by 8-foot concrete slabs. Unfortunately, they're out in the open with no sun protection.

Shortly after reaching the NAS property, the trail runs through a wide corridor. The whole corridor is quite open and exposed (or majestic, depending on your tastes) with more than 200 feet of mown lawns. At mile 8.85 you come to the fence for the NAS. There's a guardhouse on the highway to your left but no equivalent building for checking trail users.

After the fence the whole system further opens up into miles of grassy lawns and runways. In the distance ahead of you is a series of water towers and base buildings. This area could be a problem in heavy winds but is otherwise fun to experience, with those rare (for Florida) undeveloped spaces running on for miles.

At mile 9.15 is an airport taxiway. Here a sign warns you to stop if the alarm sounds, signifying an approaching plane. Pass a chemical pesticide control building sitting out all by itself before arriving at the trail terminus, among some base buildings, at mile 9.2. You can go farther on the sidewalk or roads if you are so inclined. In the future this trail is to become part of a 100-mile paved loop in the Blackwater River valley. At present, there are numerous off-road trails in the Blackwater State Forest nearby.

Rider and wild turkeys

2 Branford Trail

This trail unofficially starts at a spectacular small spring about 100 feet from the Suwannee River in an unpaved parking area. It travels a mile or so along a paved county road until it reaches the old railroad line going into Branford, which it follows to town. This small town boasts some powerful good food and a small park on the banks of the Suwannee River next to another pretty spring. Part of the Suwannee River Greenway, this short trail is a lot of fun.

Activities:

Location: Suwannee County

Length: 4.7 miles

Surface: Asphalt; 10 feet wide

Wheelchair access: Throughout its length

Difficulty: Easy

Food: There are plenty of food facilities in the center of the town of Branford and at the intersection of the trail with US 27.

Rest room facilities: At Ivey Memorial Park on US 27.

Seasons: Open all year.

Access and parking: In addition to the Little River Springs parking lot, you can park and access the trail both north and south of its intersection with US 27. You can take a Greyhound bus to Branford, but you're on your own after that.

Rentals: Dive equipment rentals are available at the shop just south of US 27.

Contact: Suwannee County Recreation Department Branford; (904) 362–3004.

• •

Sometimes it's hard to get enthusiastic about short rail-trails. Not this one! As on the Nature Coast—Fanning Springs Trail to the south, the presence of the Suwannee River overshadows you during the brief time it takes you to travel. The people of Branford have wholeheartedly supported this trail, and the local merchants want your business. Though the rail-trail portion follows a state highway into town, the trail feels quiet and serene for most of its length—until it reaches the lively activities in Branford, where the smell of barbecue permeates the air and lots of small boats are launched into the river. If you can combine a ride on this trail with a visit to any number of springs located in the area, or the 4-mile canoe trail to Branford from Little River Springs to the north, you've got a good day planned.

The railroad line now used by the trail was built in the late nineteenth century to transport local wood and farm products to state and national markets. By 1882 Branford was the terminus of the Live Oak and Rowlands Bluff Railroad at the Suwannee River. From Branford a steamboat carried goods from the Suwannee valley downriver until around 1920. The line was abandoned in the late 1960s; the paved rail trail opened in 1997.

Start this outing from the parking lot at Little River Springs 5 miles north of Branford. To reach the lot, take US 129 north out of Branford to County Road 248; turn left and drive 1.5 miles until the road dead-ends at the Suwannee River. Before you leave the parking

Suwanee River park overlook

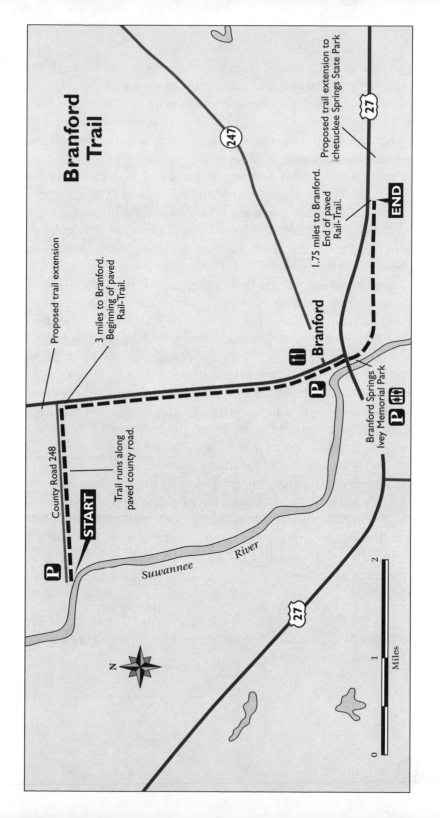

Branford Trail

Proposed trail extension

3 miles to Branford. Beginning of paved Rail-Trail.

County Road 248

Trail runs along paved county road.

START

P

P

Branford

Suwannee River

Branford Springs
Ivey Memorial Park

P

1.75 miles to Branford. End of paved Rail-Trail.

Proposed trail extension to Ichetuckee Springs State Park

END

247

27

27

N

0   1   2
Miles

lot, go look at the spring and maybe take a dip to cool off. All the springs in Florida stay at around 72 degrees year-round.

Ride back the way you drove in on County Road 248. The official paved rail-trail starts at the intersection of County Road 248 and US 129 and goes south. The unpaved abandoned rail line heads farther north but is not passable at present.

For the first mile the trail travels next to US 129 with no buffer on your left and hardwood upland hammock on your right. After a mile the trail moves a few feet to the west, where a nice buffer of trees has been established between the trail and road. This configuration continues for the next 1.6 miles, with some interspersed houses, until you reach Branford.

For about 0.5 mile the trail goes through the city of Branford with its houses, commercial establishments, and restaurants. At 3.0 miles, where you cross US 27 and pass through Ivey Memorial Park, there is a parking area with rest rooms, picnic tables, a boat ramp, and a dive concession. There are numerous places to get food and gas on US 27 at or near the trail crossing.

Next to US 27 in Ivey Park is Branford Springs, whose blue-green waters can be viewed from a boardwalk that circles the boil area. The spring run is only a few feet from the Suwannee River. It disappears under black water when the river is high, so don't be disappointed when nature does its thing at flood times.

After leaving the park, the trail passes by houses and ranchettes with fairly tall trees on each side, but no full canopy. At about 1.7 miles from US 27 the paved trail ends at a warning sign asking you not to trespass of Florida Power Corporation property. This trail will eventually become part of a longer paved trail continuing on to Ichetucknee State Park.

This short but fun urban trail travels from a mall in Orlando north to a park in Winter Park. For much of its length, it passes an old naval training base that is now owned by the city of Orlando and scheduled for future development. Because the plans are not finalized, it's difficult to predict what the trailside will look like in a few years. For now, the old base is open and getting overgrown. The rest of the trail passes apartments and medium-priced homes along a partially tree-lined trail. There are more dog walkers on this trail per mile than any other in the state by personal observation. It's very crowded on weekends, but all that activity can be exciting.

Activities:

Location: Orange County

Length: 3.6 miles

Surface: Asphalt; 12 feet wide, with some separations exclusively for walkers

Wheelchair access: Throughout its length

Difficulty: Easy

Food: Lots of food is available at the Fashion Square Mall at the southern trailhead and along Aloma Avenue in Winter Park in the north.

Rest room facilities: At Fashion Square Mall at the southern end of the trail and Cady Way Park in the northern end.

Seasons: Open all year.

Access and parking: The trail can be accessed at all trailheads and crossroads. Orlando Transit Authority will get you close.

Rentals: N/A.

Contact: Orange County Parks and Recreation; (407) 836–6200.

• •

A good short ride in the greater Orlando Area, the Cady Way Trail will ultimately connect with the Cross Seminole Trail (see Trail 5) to the north and become an important part of the Central Florida Loop. It's worth riding on a Saturday or Sunday afternoon just to see how many different types of people use rail-trails.

The trail is built on the former rail bed of the Seaboard Coastline Railroad. The railroad was mainly used for local traffic until it was abandoned in the 1980s. The rail trail was acquired by the City of Orlando and paved in 1994. It was the city's first multiuse trail facility.

Find the Fashion Square Mall on east State Road 50 (Colonial Drive) in Orlando and go to the northeastern corner of the parking lot. Here you will find the southern trailhead for the Cady Way Trail with covered picnic facilities and water fountains.

The trail beginning is well designated, and mile markers appear every 0.5 mile. There is water at each trailhead and at three additional locations along the trail, about a mile apart. This trail also has the only doggi-pot waste pickup facility we've seen on a rail-trail in Florida, a much-needed addition in light of the number of dog walkers.

As you leave the parking area, the trail passes through a light commercial area and across a long wooden bridge at Lake Gear at mile 0.25. The Orlando Naval Training Center is to your left for the first 0.5 mile until you travel through a middle-income residential area. There are lots of crossroads, but blue markings and stripes get you across.

At mile 1.5 you pass a water treatment plant and the continuation of the Naval Training Center on your left. To your right are residential areas until you come to the golf course at mile 2.25.

At mile 2.8 you pass the xeriscape memorial garden (dedicated by Rollins College students to one of their own) and the doggi-pot. There are drainage canals on both sides of the trail and a full tree canopy at mile 3.0. From here you pass residential areas all the way to the Cady Way Park, a full facility local park with rest rooms, picnic areas, tennis courts, and parking.

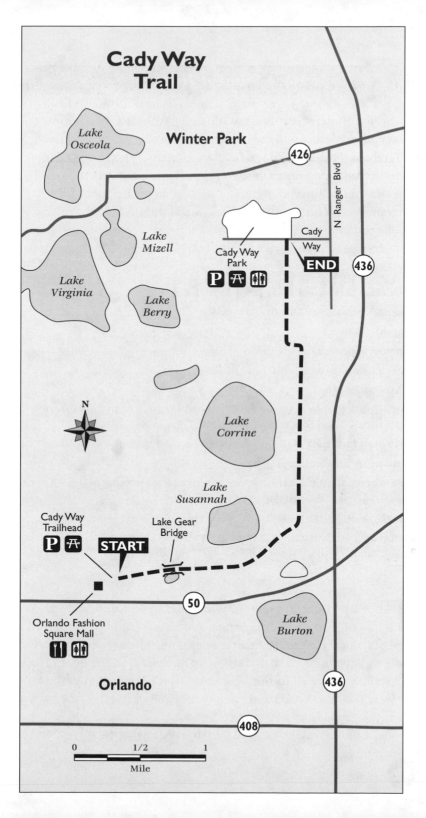

Cady Way Trail

Winter Park

Lake Osceola

426

N Ranger Blvd

Lake Mizell

Cady Way Park

Cady Way

END

436

Lake Virginia

Lake Berry

N

Lake Corrine

Lake Susannah

Cady Way Trailhead

Lake Gear Bridge

START

50

Lake Burton

Orlando Fashion Square Mall

Orlando

436

408

0   1/2   1

Mile

4 Cape Haze Pioneer Trail

This is a trail in creation. It's one of the first parts of a planned supersystem that will eventually include the Gasparilla Island Trail and the old bridges to Gasparilla Island. The trail is northeast of the large Rotunda development through an area that's now mainly cow pasture, but it'll be filled with housing developments in the near future. The trail is a straight shot with no hills or curves.

Activities:

Location: Charlotte County

Length: 3.8 miles

Surface: Asphalt; 8 feet wide

Wheelchair access: Throughout its length

Difficulty: Easy

Food: You'll find food in the Charlotte Beach area, at the intersection of State Road 776 and Secondary State Road 771.

Rest room facilities: None yet, but some are planned at the trailhead.

Seasons: Open all year.

Access and parking: There is a new trailhead with parking at the corner of State Road 776 and Secondary State Road 771.

Rentals: N/A.

Contact: Charlotte County Parks and Recreation Department, 4500 Harbor Boulevard, Port Charlotte, FL 33952–9171; (941) 743–1313.

• • • • • • • • • • • • • • • • • • • •

The Cape Haze Pioneer Trail is straight-line romp adjacent to a line of palm trees, pine trees, palmettos, and open fields that were once part of a coastal cattle operation. The area is now developing rapidly and will be an oasis among houses in the near future. By itself it's a nice short outing, but when it's connected to the larger system over to Gasparilla Island (see Trail 9) it'll become part of an exciting mainland-to-beach trailway.

The Charlotte Harbor and Northern Railway (a subsidiary of

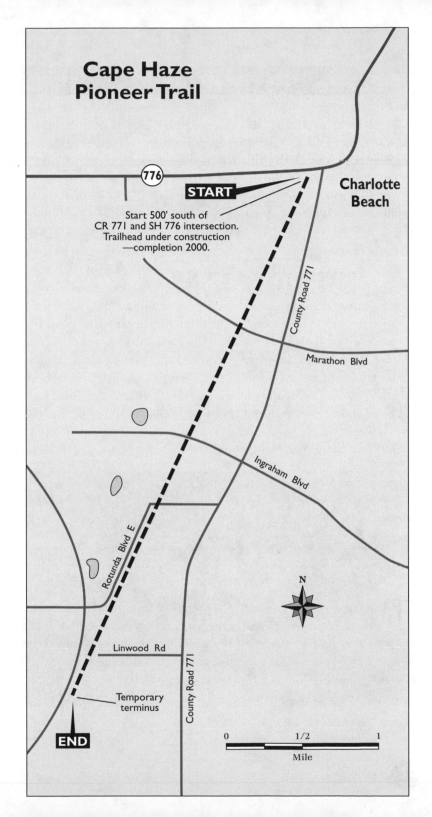

Cape Haze Pioneer Trail

776

START

Start 500' south of CR 771 and SH 776 intersection. Trailhead under construction —completion 2000.

Charlotte Beach

County Road 771

Marathon Blvd

Ingraham Blvd

Rotunda Blvd E

N

Linwood Rd

County Road 771

Temporary terminus

END

0   1/2   1
Mile

American Agricultural Chemical Company) was built in 1907 to carry lumber and phosphate rock by ship from Boca Grande to world markets. It connected with a line that went east to Fort Ogden and Hull on its way to Acadia, 49 miles inland. Another portion of this line was connected to Plant City to the northeast (see Trail 10, the Gen. James A. Van Fleet). In 1917 the Charlotte Harbor and Northern Railway owned 217 freight cars, fifteen passenger cars, and fifty-six units of work equipment. The line was acquired in 1928 by Seaboard Airline Railroad, which operated the system until 1982; then it was abandoned. The land was acquired from Seaboard by Charlotte County, and the first phase of the trail was opened in 1999.

Start your outing at the new trailhead at the corner of State Road 776 and Secondary State Road 771. From there you travel along a straight path with a few houses interspersed along old pasturelands. Scattered about the fields are the occasional clump of pine trees and palmettos, along with a few houses. The highway is to your left, and the large Rotunda development is to your right. You'll pass occasional ponds in the drainage ways and salt marshes that contain wading birds and small mammals. The trail ends just south of Linwood Road next to the Rotunda development. The second phase of this trail to the south is already past the planning stage and should be constructed in the next few years. The connection to Gasparilla Island will be next.

Along the Cape Haze Pioneer Trail

This is a developing trail that will become part of a larger system to be constructed over the next few years. It runs from the town of Winter Springs in the east to Oviedo in the west along a series of upscale subdivisions. With the old railroad right-of-way thickly vegetated with large trees on both sides, there's a peacefulness to this trail that's often missing on urban trails. Add some running creek water and an interesting bridge or two and this is fun place to ride.

Activities:

Location: Seminole County

Length: 3.5 miles

Surface: Asphalt; 12 feet wide

Wheelchair access: Throughout its length

Difficulty: Easy

Food: There is plenty of food and lodging in downtown Oviedo and along State Road 434 east and west of the Black Hammock Trailhead.

Rest room facilities: Rest rooms are available in commercial establishments in Oviedo; they're planned for the Black Hammock Trailhead in the future.

Seasons: Open all year.

Access and parking: Found at the Black Hammock Trailhead, in downtown Oviedo, and at crossroads along the way. There's some local bus service; check with the Seminole County Transit.

Rentals: N/A.

Contact: Seminole County Parks and Recreation, 264 West North Street, Altamonte Springs, FL 32714; (407) 788–0405.

• • • • • • • • • • • • • • • • • • • •

This is another fun little urban trail, but it's an upscale version. It's by far one of the best-landscaped rail-trails in the state. The intersections are divided with planting of coontie ferns inside cement planters. The trail has distance markers on small signs opposite each other at 0.25-mile intervals (which is disconcerting for

A good place to see spawning alligator garfish at the Howell Creek Trestle

bicyclists traveling at speed, but probably fine for walkers). At various places along the trail, off-road bike and horse trails head a few yards off the paved trail into the wooded right-of-way for a few hundred yards before coming back to the paved trail or crossing over.

The trail is built in a former local railroad corridor that was used to transport vegetables in the Sanford-Orlando area before being abandoned when trucks became more prevalent. The Black Hammock Trailhead is on a spur. The land was purchased by the Department of Environmental Protection Office of Greenways and Trails and opened as a rail-trail in 1998.

Starting at the Winter Springs end, the trail travels between upscale homes for 0.7 mile before it reaches a wonderful original train trestle over Howell Creek. The trestle has been restored with wooden sides and a cement surface. It's a good place to hang down and look into the creek for the large garfish that populate the area.

From there the trail follows a drainage creek and lush wetlands vegetation as it passes adjacent homes. At mile 1.5 the trail passes the first Black Hammock Trailhead cutoff to your left; a second appears a few hundred yards farther on. The trailhead is on a short

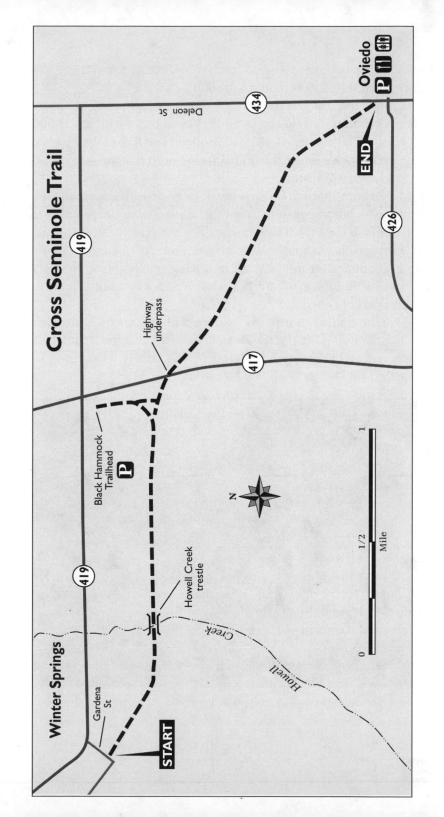

Cross Seminole Trail

Winter Springs

Oviedo

419

419

434 Deleon St

417

426

Black Hammock Trailhead

P

Highway underpass

Howell Creek trestle

Gardena St

START

END

Howell Creek

N

0   1/2   1
Mile

(0.5-mile) former spur line and has covered picnic areas as well as parking and water. Rest rooms will soon be added.

Between the Howell Creek bridge and Black Hammock, there are a number of unpaved side trails off the paved trail for off-road bikes and horses. This section is newly developed and will probably need some breaking in, but it should be a good outing when it's done if the trail surface is maintained.

In this area there are also a number of private small wooden bridges, which homeowners have built across the drainage creek to gain access to the trail. Though these are not exactly legal, they do add a certain charm, and may or may not remain depending on future negotiations. At mile 2.0 the trail passes under State Road 417 and travels through a relatively undeveloped area until it reaches the outskirts of Oviedo.

Here the trail has a nice tree canopy with houses on both sides. The temporary end of the trail is in downtown Oviedo, with lots of restaurants and food service. Eventually this trail will become part of the Central Florida Loop.

A sheltered rest spot at the Black Hammock Trailhead

This is an urban trail going through central Gainesville. It passes through and on the edges of a number of neighborhoods and industrial areas.

Activities:

Location: Alachua County

Length: 2.1 miles

Surface: Asphalt; 10 feet wide.

Wheelchair access: Throughout its length

Difficulty: Easy

Food: State Road 26 and US 441 offer places to get food.

Rest room facilities: Soon to be opened at the old train depot in the downtown industrial area.

Seasons: Open all year.

Access and parking: At crossroads. The local transit authority will take you to a number of locations along the trail.

Rentals: N/A.

Contact: Linda B. Dixon, City of Gainesville Public Works Department, Station 58, P.O. Box 490, Gainesville, FL 32602–0490; (352) 334–5074.

• •

This short urban trail is used as much by commuters as it is by recreational users. This will change when the trail system for the area is completed, allowing you to travel around urban Gainesville or head to the rural parks to the south and east of town. It's a pleasant trail that old railroad buffs will certainly enjoy because of the newly renovated old depot and the connection with the industrial areas. It adjoins the Waldo Road Greenway at its northeastern terminus.

This trail was a CSX Transportation rail line into the 1980s. It served downtown Gainesville before the passenger terminal was moved to the northeastern part of town on Waldo Road. It was then used as a siding for industrial deliveries until it was abandoned.

The bike-pedestrian bridge over US 441 near the University of Florida campus

The trail starts across the highway from the Shands Teaching Hospital on the University of Florida campus and crosses US 441 on an old train trestle. (There is no designated parking except along the streets.) From there it continues under a tree canopy through various neighborhoods until it reaches an open industrial area by the old train depot. The depot is being refurbished as a trailhead; when it's completed, over the next few years, it will be a fun stop for food and rest. After you pass through the industrial area, the trail once more is covered by a tree canopy and passes through neighborhoods of east Gainesville until it comes out at its terminus on busy, commercial University Avenue.

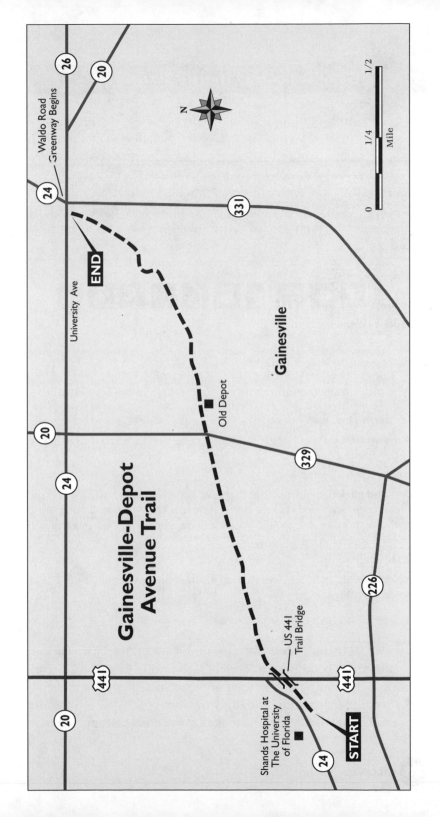

Gainesville-Depot Avenue Trail

Waldo Road
Greenway Begins

University Ave

END

24

26

20

331

Gainesville

Old Depot

20

24

329

441

US 441
Trail Bridge

226

441

Shands Hospital at
The University
of Florida

24

START

N

0   1/4   1/2

Mile

This is a wonderful trail through some of the best natural areas in north-central Florida. It's wooded and quiet even though it travels close to busy highways and country roads. All of the 15-plus miles are a pleasure to travel, and there are even a few hills to climb and speed down. If you take your time and visit some of the Paynes Prairie Preserve's La Chua Trail, you'll have an opportunity to see bison, wild horses, and sandhill cranes.

Activities:

Location: Alachua County

Length: 15 miles

Surface: Asphalt; 10 feet wide

Wheelchair access: Throughout its length, including accessible rest rooms

Difficulty: Easy

Food: You can find places to eat in Gainesville and along US 301 in Hawthorne.

Rest room facilities: Available at Bulware Springs City Park and the Lochloosa and Hawthorne Trailheads.

Seasons: Open all year.

Access and parking: Bulware Springs City Park; County Road 234; and the La Chua, Lochloosa, and Hawthorne Trailheads. The Alachua County Transit Authority may be able to help you with transportation. Otherwise talk to the local Gainesville bike shops.

Rentals: N/A.

Contact: Florida Park Service, Paynes Prairie State Preserve, Route 2, Box 41, Micanopy, FL 32667.

• •

This is a mainly rural trail from Bulware Springs City Park in the urban southeastern area of Gainesville to the small community of Hawthorne farther east. It passes next to a state preserve and a wildlife management area, which are both good for wildlife viewing. The small ranchettes along the way don't intrude much on

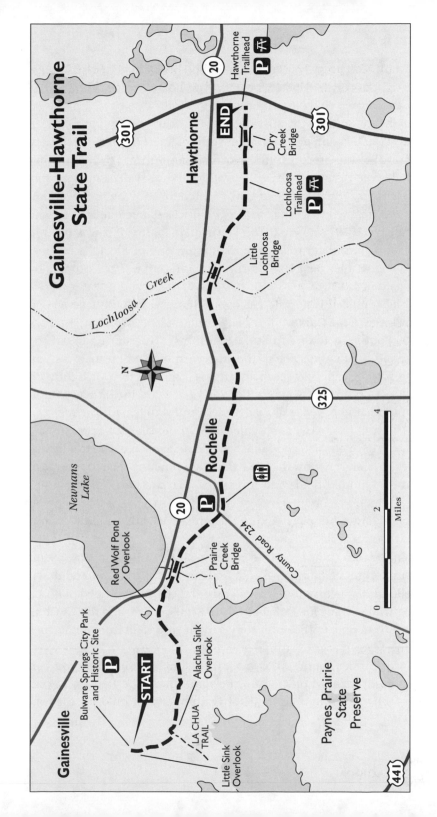

this trail, with its graceful wooden arched bridges over small creeks. The right-of-way is wide enough for safe horse passage but still has substantial tree coverage adjacent to the trail.

Bulware Springs City Park at the Gainesville-Hawthorne Trailhead is the location of the original settlement of Gainesville, founded in 1854. It's presently the western beginning of the trail and includes the historic Gainesville waterworks as well as modern picnic facilities. The railroad line over which most of the trail was constructed traveled from this area to what was to become Hawthorne starting in 1879. Known as the Peninsular Railroad, it was used to transport phosphate rock to market from one of Florida's earliest phosphate mines near Hawthorne. The rail-trail was constructed by the state in 1992.

The trailhead is not the easiest to find if you don't have a good knowledge of the Gainesville area. Start at Bulware Springs City Park (3300 Southeast Fifteenth Street, on the southeastern edge of the city) and follow the signs to the trail west of the entrance. As you approach the trail, you'll see an unpaved section to your right with an arrow pointing to Gainesville. You *don't* want to go that way. To your left is the paved trail that goes 15 miles to Hawthorne.

The trail has markers on poles every mile that are generally accurate. There are also good maps available at each of the trailheads.

As you start off on the trail there's a housing development on your left and old fields and forestland that are part of the Paynes Prairie State Preserve (see page 130) to your right. At 0.7 mile you climb a gentle hill overlooking the preserve with a nice view out over the prairie.

Equestrian trails cross the paved trail from time to time. Soon the trail enters a hammock area and actually curves up and down wooded hills, where it deviates from the old railroad bed. The La Chua Trail parking lot is at about the 0.9-mile mark, and the La Chua Nature Trail (foot traffic only) comes in on your right from the Paynes Prairie State Preserve at mile 1.3.

At 1.7 miles there's an overview of Alachua Sink that you can reach from a paved offshoot of the main trail. The Red Wolf Pond Overlook appears at mile 4.1. Shortly afterward, at mile 4.4, the trail

Arched bridges span the creeks for bike riders

parallels the very busy State Road 20 for a short stretch before turning south back into less noisy and more natural habitat.

At mile 4.8 is the Prairie Creek Bridge, one of a number of gently arched wooden bridges on the trail. Horses that are traveling along the side of the trail are directed over the bridge at this point, or through the water in a ford next to it.

At mile 5.0 the trail parallels County Road 2082. At mile 6.4 there's a parking area next to the trail where County Road 234 crosses. There is a fair amount of shade along this section except when the sun is directly overhead.

At mile 6.6 is a pit toilet serving trail users. At mile 7.5 the Lochloosa Wildlife Management Area starts, and you are warned about ongoing hunting during the season. This is a mixed pine-hardwood area of once-cut forest that is managed by the Florida Fish and Wildlife Commission for hunting from November through January.

You cross the Little Lochloosa Bridge at mile 10.2. After passing through the management area at 192nd Street, you come to the small rural community of Grove Park at 11.2 miles. This is the location of Pete's Bike and Air, which offers repairs, air for your tires, and water for thirsty riders.

Cross over the Lochloosa Creek Bridge at mile 11.8 and reenter the wildlife management area at mile 12.8. At mile 13.9 is the Lochloosa Trailhead (7209 Southeast 200th Drive) with paved parking, picnic tables, water, and interpretive signs. The trail crosses the Dry Creek Bridge at mile 14.7 and proceeds to its end in Hawthorne across from the Hawthorne Junior-Senior High School at mile 15.2. The Hawthorne Trailhead (300 Southwest Second Avenue) has picnic tables, water, and interpretive signs. Driving into Hawthorne, plenty of informative brown directional signs lead you from US 301 to this trailhead.

This is an urban trail along a major thoroughfare in eastern Gainesville. It passes near the road and along the edges of a number of neighborhoods. Funded as a landscaped park for beautification purposes, it features wonderful landscaping and flowers.

Activities:

Location: Alachua County

Length: 2.6 miles

Surface: Asphalt; 10 feet wide

Wheelchair access: Throughout its length

Difficulty: Easy

Food: Look for food along State Roads 26, 24, and 222.

Rest room facilities: None.

Seasons: Open all year.

Access and parking: At crossroads. The local transit authority will take you to a number of locations along the trail.

Rentals: N/A.

Contact: Linda B. Dixon, City of Gainesville Public Works Department, Station 58, P.O. Box 490, Gainesville, FL 32602–0490; (352) 334–5074.

• • • • • • • • • • • • • • • • • • • •

This former CSX Transportation rail line was abandoned in the 1980s. The rail-trail was developed in the mid-1990s as part of a beautification project rather than solely for recreationalists. For this reason it has better landscaping than most trails and contains a number of comfortable benches and nooks along the way.

Begin at the northeastern corner of University Avenue and State Road 24 at the eastern end of Gainesville's commercial district. For its whole length the trail travels next to State Road 24, until it ends

Along the Gainesville–Waldo Road Greenway

at State Road 222. It's a nice straight shot from end to end, with lots of planted flowers, trees, and shrubs blooming at various times of the year. Once a blighted railroad corridor, it now boasts plenty of users who enjoy the beautiful vegetation along the way.

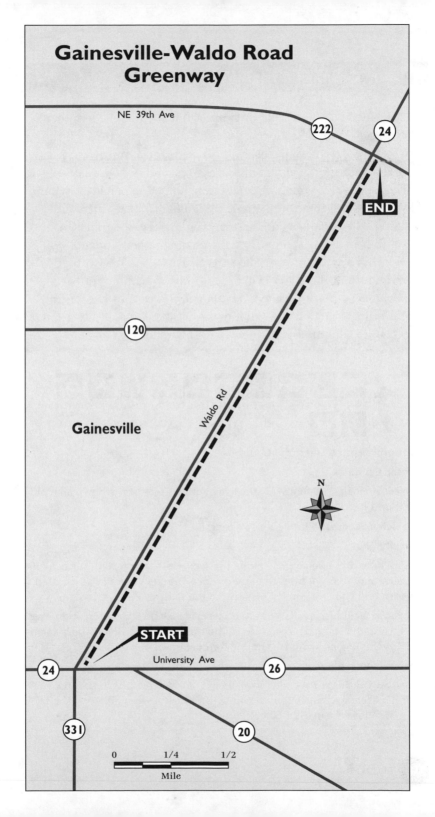

Gainesville-Waldo Road Greenway

NE 39th Ave

222 24

END

120

Gainesville

Waldo Rd

N

START

University Ave

24 26

331 20

0   1/4   1/2
Mile

9 Gasparilla Island Trail

This was the first rail-trail built in Florida. It runs the length of Gasparilla Island on Florida's southwestern coast through the town of Boca Grande. Gasparilla Island is a semitropical paradise filled with the homes of wealthy residents who care deeply about their trail. Traveling past stately homes, expensive shops, swaying palm trees, and streaking iguanas makes this a great outing. The terrain is flat, the vegetation next to the trail is lush, and there's always something interesting to see. Indeed, you won't have an opportunity to travel past so much wealth anywhere else in the state. Don't expect cheap hamburgers or an inexpensive place to sleep. The beach is free, but everything else reflects the local population. You even have to pay a toll ($3.50) to get onto the island in the first place.

Activities:

Location: Lee and Charlotte Counties

Length: 6.5 miles

Surface: Asphalt; a 10-foot-wide roadway with a 4-foot pedestrian trail winding around it

Wheelchair access: Throughout its length

Difficulty: Easy

Food: There are food sources along the trail, with one restaurant near its southern end, many within the city of Boca Grande, and one at the trail's northern end: Uncle Henry's Restaurant and Lodge.

Rest room facilities: Available at the Gasparilla Island State Recreation Area just beyond the southern terminus of the trail, and at some business establishments in downtown Boca Grande for customers.

Seasons: Open all year.

Access and parking: Parking is available at the trail's southern end, the public beach accesses near town, the cross streets in town, and along the trail where it follows Gasparilla Island Boulevard.

Rentals: N/A.

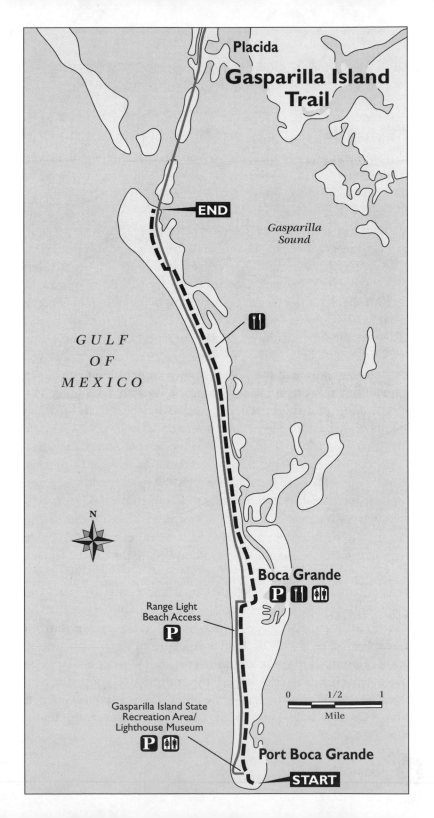

Placida

Gasparilla Island Trail

END

Gasparilla Sound

GULF OF MEXICO

N

Boca Grande

Range Light Beach Access

Gasparilla Island State Recreation Area/ Lighthouse Museum

0   1/2   1
Mile

Port Boca Grande

START

Contact: Lee County Department of Transportation, 2022 Hendry Street, Fort Myers, FL 33901; (813) 335–2220.

• •

This is a pleasant romp on a tropical island, but what will most catch your eye are the ever-present iguanas that dart back and forth along the trail. Yes, I did say "iguanas"! For the last twenty-five years, this island has been the home of the spiny-tailed iguana, an exotic lizard that grows up to $3^1/_2$ feet long. These iguanas are the descendants of released or escaped former pets. In warmer weather you can expect these big lizards to dart in front of you unexpectedly anywhere on the trail. They don't seem to bother anyone, but they do take a bit of getting used to. Don't try to feed or otherwise mess with them, though, because they have been known to become somewhat aggressive.

This was the first rail-trail conversion in Florida, built in the 1980s. The island, which gives the trail its name, was named for José Gaspar, a notorious pirate of the 1700s who was reputed to hang out in the area after his raids on coastal communities and shipping. The Calusa Indians and their predecessors were probably the first inhabitants of the island, dating back many thousands of years. Much of the Gasparilla Island Trail is built on the former bed of the Charlotte Harbor and Northern Railway (a subsidiary of American Agricultural Chemical Company), built in 1907 to carry lumber and phosphate rock by ship from Boca Grande to world markets. It connected with a line across the bridges from the island to the east to Fort Ogden and Hull on its way to Acadia, 49 miles inland. Another portion of this line was connected to Plant City to the northeast (see Trail 10, Gen. James A. Van Fleet). In 1917 the Charlotte Harbor and Northern Railway owned 217 freight cars, fifteen passenger cars and fifty-six units of work equipment. The line was acquired in 1928 by the Seaboard Airline Railroad, which operated the system until it was abandoned in 1982. The land was acquired from Seaboard by Charlotte County, and the first phase of the trail was opened in 1989.

Because this is a narrow island, the trail follows the main road (Gasparilla Road) from one end to the other. There is no way to miss this trail! The best way to experience this trail is to start at the southern end at Gasparilla Island State Recreation Area and travel out and back so that you can swim and shower when you return. You can also tour the lighthouse and museum in the recreation area.

One unusual thing about this trail (other than the iguanas) is the number of golf carts using it. This is the only trail we've ever used that permits golf carts, which seem to be the most common users on weekdays. They're supposed to yield to bikes and pedestrians, but be careful anyway.

The trail actually starts across Belcher Road from the recreation area driveway. From there it travels along Gulf Boulevard and the Gulf of Mexico beaches to your left for a mile before it takes a sharp right turn into the town of Boca Grand on First Street.

Before you reach the turnoff, you pass a big steel range light next to one of the two public beach access points. It's an interesting structure that substitutes for a lighthouse when operational. It makes for good photo ops.

Numerous streets cross the trail from Gulf Boulevard on your right, but the curbs are smooth enough for handicapped users and not much of a problem. When you turn onto First Street, you travel on a small sidewalk for a block or two before turning left back onto

The Gasparilla Island Lighthouse and Museum

the trail. From this point, you pass through downtown Boca Grande in a beautifully landscaped and shaded area of the trail that takes you by good food and shops for a 0.5 mile until you come out on a grassy verge between the main road (Gasparilla Road) and the residential areas to the east.

At this point a pedestrian-only trail starts alongside. It's composed of gravel with cement borders, and it winds around the paved trail all the way to the northern end. The grass area ends in about 3 miles where the trail crosses over to the western side of Gasparilla Road, 0.5 mile before it ends.

On the eastern side of the road is a strip shopping center that offers food and the only reasonably priced lodging on the island (Uncle Henry's). This island has some of the highest-priced real estate in the country. Be happy for anything resembling "reasonable" here. Your other options are across the bridge to the north and on to any number of small towns on the mainland.

The trail ends at the bridge to Cole Key, just north of Gasparilla Island, with great views of the water on both sides. To the east you can see the old bridges that one day will be converted to trails that allow you to travel to the mainland and connect with the Cape Haze Pioneer Trail (see Trail 4), 3 miles north at Placida. For now, turn around and go back for a swim.

Lush tropical vegetation on the Gasparilla Island Trail in downtown Boca Grande

The Van Fleet Trail is Florida's most rural trail. It runs through what is left of the great Green Swamp, a natural water-storage area just west of the high sandy ridge that divides the state. This is the headwaters for some of Florida's most often-canoed rivers: the Withlacoochee, Hillsborough, Peace, Oklawaha, and Little Withlacoochee. Though much of the Green Swamp has been drained for citrus groves and cattle ranching, a few large tracts remain, and this trail goes right through them. Its average elevation is higher than any other rail-trail in Florida—around 100 feet above sea level—but don't expect this to be reflected in any sizable hills, because there aren't any. With only one curve in its 29.2 miles, you can choose to go slow and view the wildlife or travel as fast as you can hold it. Though this trail has a great reputation for wildlife viewing between Green Pond Road and Bay Lake Road, recent studies are giving it extra high marks for butterfly populations along its length.

Activities:

Location: Lake, Polk, and Sumter Counties

Length: 29.2 miles

Surface: Asphalt; 12 feet wide

Wheelchair access: Throughout its length

Difficulty: Easy

Food: You can find food at the southern terminus in Polk City and possibly at Bay Lake Road (1 mile east).

Rest room facilities: Full rest room facilities are available across the street from the Polk City Trailhead at the local park, as well as at the Green Pond Road and Mabel Trailheads.

Seasons: Open all year.

Access and parking: Available at the Polk City, Bay Lake, and Mabel Trailheads. There may be Greyhound Bus service to Polk City, but Mabel is just a name on the highway. Don't plan to use public transportation to arrive at or leave this trail.

Rentals: N/A.

Contact: Florida Park Service, 12549 State Park Drive, Clermont, FL 34711–8667.

• • • • • • • • • • • • • • • • • • • •

The Gen. James A. Van Fleet State Trail runs from the small town of Polk City at its southern end to the even smaller community of Mabel at its northern end. Prepare yourself for rural Florida. With only one curve along its entire length and few hills to speak of, this trail will either bore you to tears or cause endless fascination as your mind enters one of those zones that displaces time and space. For one of the few times on a rail-trail in Florida, you will escape traffic noises; the loudest sounds here are your tires spinning on the asphalt, the braying of an occasional cow, and the high call of the red-shouldered hawks that are common in this area. There is one 10-mile stretch with no crossroads and few indications of human habitation beyond the trail itself.

Mileages are painted on the trail at regular intervals in both miles and kilometers. There are lots of possibilities along this trail for great birding and wildlife viewing if you hit it right. From slow-moving gopher tortoises munching grass along the trail to white-tailed deer bounding off into the swamp, you can't be sure from moment to moment what animals you'll meet up close and personal. You could see bobcat or otters moving around at dawn or dusk looking for a meal or watering hole, or wild turkeys feasting on acorns or roosting in tall trees on the trailside.

During hunting season (Thanksgiving through mid-February) you should wear bright colors and sing a lot. There are no reports of users getting shot or shot at by errant hunters along this or any other trail, but it pays to be careful.

At the northern terminus at State Road 50, you'll find yourself in the middle of what used to be Florida's citrus belt (this has now moved farther south to avoid winter freezes). In the future this trail will connect to the Withlacoochee (see Trail 17) in the west and the Lake Minneola (see Trail 12) and West Orange (see Trail 16) in the east, all as part of the Central Florida Loop.

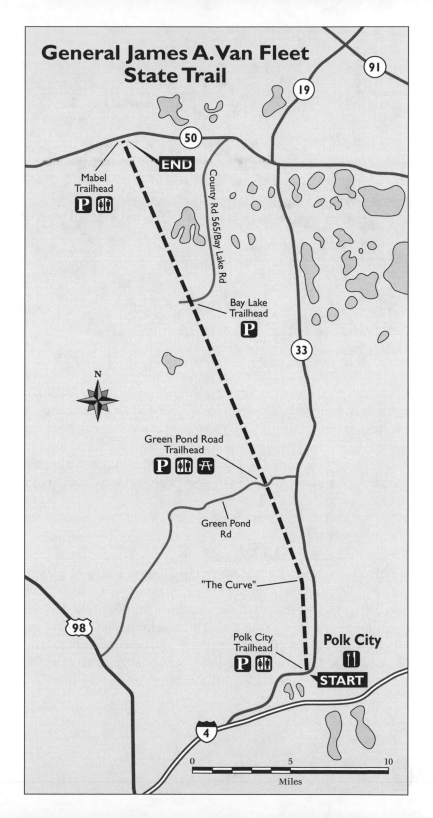

General James A. Van Fleet State Trail

91

19

50

END

Mabel
Trailhead
P 🚻

County Rd 565/Bay Lake Rd

Bay Lake
Trailhead
P

33

N

Green Pond Road
Trailhead
P 🚻 🏕

Green Pond
Rd

98

"The Curve"

Polk City
Trailhead
P 🚻

Polk City
🍴
START

4

0   5   10
Miles

The Polk City Trailhead

This trail was built on a former CSX rail line that was originally constructed in the late 1800s as part of a phosphate mining and citrus transportation network. Trains were replaced by trucks in the 1950s and 1960s, and the line was abandoned by the mid-1980s. The trail corridor was acquired by the state in 1991, and the first phase of the paved trail was completed in 1995. The entire trail was paved in 1997.

The Van Fleet Trail starts at State Road 33 and County Road 665 as it enters Polk City to the south. There are nice brown signs leading to the trail as you come off a large overpass. The trailhead is below and to the northeast of the overpass. There is plenty of parking in an open field but no other amenities. Across County Road 665 is a Polk City park with rest rooms and water if you need them.

As you start down the trail, you'll almost immediately leave the few houses around Polk City. From there you pass medium to large cattle ranches with swamps, open fields, and pine forests for the first 8 or 9 miles. Houses and trailers are clustered around the three dirt crossroads (soon to be paved), but the only really distinctive feature is "The Curve" at mile 5.0—the only one on the trail.

There is a full-facility trailhead at Green Pond Road (rest rooms, water, parking, and covered picnic tables). From here to Bay Lake Loop Trailhead, you'll pass large flatwoods ranch pastures, forests, hardwood and cypress swamps, 10 miles with no crossroads, and little human habitation. The Green Swamp with the Green Swamp and Richloam Wildlife Management Areas are mainly on the western side, with large ranches and an occasional house to the east. This is the headwaters of many major rivers. You'll cross three cement bridges just north of Green Pond spaced less than a mile apart.

You'll find a parking area and a few houses in the Bay Lake Loop area, as well as a small general store a mile to the east. Patrons of the store can use the rest rooms.

From Bay Lake the trail continues through similar habitat until it reaches the Mabel terminus at State Road 50 in what used to be the heart of Florida citrus country. There are four small wooden bridges between Mabel and Bay Lake, but they don't intrude on the serenity of your trip. You'll find a few citrus groves about 4 miles from Mabel on the eastern side of the trail. The trailhead at Mabel has full facilities, but the nearest food is 5 miles away in either direction on State Road 50.

The Jacksonville–Baldwin Rail-Trail is one big surprise from beginning to end. Running from the highly urbanized Jacksonville to the bedroom community of Baldwin, you would expect an urban trail with lots of noise and commotion. Nothing is farther from the truth! This trail is downright serene. It travels through woodlands most of the way, with only a few houses at widely interspersed intervals. Even with I–4 only a few miles to the south, traffic noise is at a minimum unless the wind is from the right direction—and that's rare for this area.

Activities:

Length: 14.5 miles

Surface: Asphalt; 12 feet wide

Wheelchair access: Throughout its length

Difficulty: Easy

Food: Available in Jacksonville at Commonwealth Boulevard and I–295, and on US 90 in Baldwin.

Rest room facilities: Found at Baldwin Visitors Center.

Seasons: Open all year.

Access and parking: You can access the trail at the Brandy Branch Road Trailhead, the Baldwin Visitors Center, and Ingram Road Trailhead. You can take a Greyhound Bus to Baldwin. The Jacksonville Transit Authority provides in-town transportation.

Rentals: N/A.

Contact: City of Jacksonville Parks, Recreation and Entertainment Department, 555 West Forty-Fourth Street, Jacksonville, FL 32208; (904) 630–5400.

• • • • • • • • • • • • • • • • • • • •

This is a fine rural outing on a flat, mostly straight rail-trail. It goes through pine-palmetto forest, passing a few small ranches and private residences. Even though you're adjacent to a very populated area, it's a quiet trail with few busy, intrusive crossroads. The

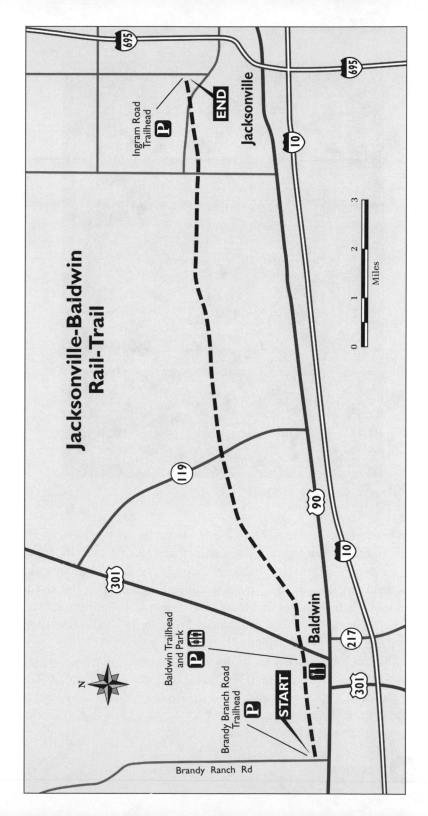

Jacksonville-Baldwin
Rail-Trail

695

695

Jacksonville

10

Ingram Road
Trailhead
P

END

Miles
0   1   2   3

119

90

10

301

N

Baldwin Trailhead
and Park
P

217

Brandy Branch Road
Trailhead
P

START

Baldwin

301

Brandy Ranch Rd

Riding through the pine forest

trailhead is well marked from US 90 and easy to find. There are mileage markers every mile on the northern side of the trail, showing the distance from the Jacksonville end. The dirt crossroads that pass over the trail have all been stabilized with asphalt out to the right-of-way line (50 feet on either side of the trail's centerline). This keeps the cross traffic from dragging dirt onto the trail or breaking down the edges of the asphalt.

This trail was once part of the CSX Transportation line, which was purchased by the state in 1992. The trail was opened in 1999 by the Office of Greenways and Trails at the Department of Environmental Protection and turned over to the city of Jacksonville for management a few months later.

If you decide to start at its western end, the trail departs from the stabilized parking lot trailhead off Secondary State Road 121 (Brandy Branch Road). You can get there by taking exit 50 north off I-10 to US 90 in Baldwin. Turn right onto Secondary State Road 121, 2 miles west of town.

After leaving the parking lot, the trail starts off on an 8-foot raised rail bed, passing ranchettes and some wet hammock for its first 2 miles until you reach the town of Baldwin at mile 12.5 from Jacksonville (again, mileage is measured from the Jacksonville end). At the edge of town is a parking area with a small city park containing swings, rest room facilities, ball fields, and similar amenities.

As you leave Baldwin, you cross an active railroad line and pass under the US 301 bridge. At mile 11.5 you enter a major riverine wetland hammock of large mature trees that shade the trail, though the water level will vary greatly depending on recent on rainfall.

After passing through the swampy area, the trail moves into an area of planted pines and large mature trees left within the right-of-way. At mile 7.6 a dirt road goes off to the north into a hunting management area—which could make a nice side trip when hunting isn't going on. There is tree cover on most of the trail and good shade as long as the sun is not directly overhead. There is some full canopy but not much.

There are few if any structures near the trail from mile 10.5 to mile 6.4. It's mostly pine forest with some open fields that were once cattle ranches. Mile 5.8 starts another riverine floodplain, and at mile 5.6 the trail crosses McGirts Creek on a nice wooden bridge. There also appear to be some off-road trails that take off next to the bridge, but they may not be authorized.

Coming out of the floodplain, ranchettes start appearing to the south, with substantial woodlands to the north. At mile 3.5 ranchettes and trailers became commonplace, though there is still a substantial tree buffer on both sides of the trail in most places. You also pick up a major power line that follows the trail from mile 3.0 to the Ingram Road Trailhead. If you listen carefully you can hear the wires singing as you breeze along. The Ingram Road Trailhead has substantial parking but no other facilities.

12 Lake Minneola Scenic State Trail/ Clermont Trail

Though these were actually constructed as separate trails, one is a direct continuation of the other along the same lake and so, for convenience, we'll treat them as a single trail in this guide. This is a very pleasant, mostly urban trail, with higher hills than any other rail-trail in Florida. The lake views on the western side are spectacular at sunset and very pretty the rest of the time. Though it's open to high winds during storms, this is a nice trail no matter what your level of experience and will become particularly attractive for long trips once it's connected to the West Orange Trail (see Trail 16) in the east and the Gen. James A. Van Fleet State Trail (see Trail 10) in the west. This is also one of the few trails that features streetlights on most portions.

Activities:

Location: Lake County

Length: 3.1 miles

Surface: Asphalt; 14 feet wide

Wheelchair access: Throughout its length

Difficulty: Easy

Food: On US 27 in Minneola there is fast food, gas, and restaurants. Along the trail in Clermont you'll find an ice cream store and restaurant near the western end of the trail. Downtown Clermont is up the hill 2 blocks south of the trail and has all the amenities.

Rest room facilities: Available at the Minneola and both Clermont Trailheads.

Seasons: Open all year.

Access and parking: Available at all trailheads and crossroads.

Rentals: In Clermont

Contact: Lake County Public Works, Engineering Division, 123 North Sinclair Avenue, Tavares, FL 32778; (352) 235–4900.

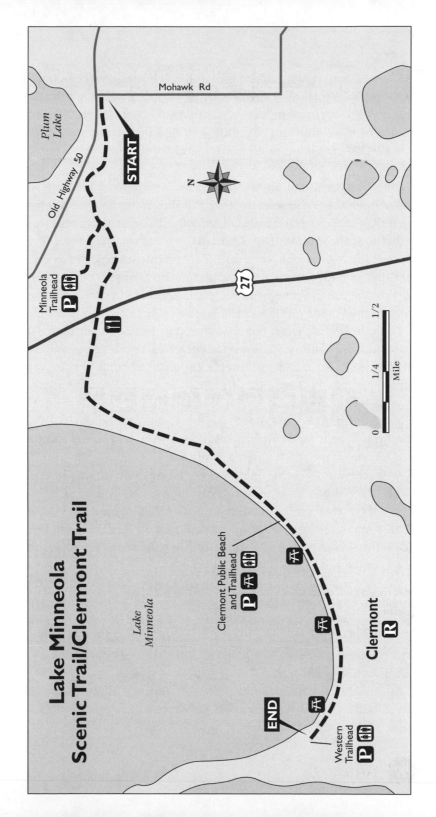

Lake Minneola
Scenic Trail/Clermont Trail

Mohawk Rd

Plum Lake

Old Highway 50

START

N

Minneola Trailhead

27

Lake Minneola

Clermont Public Beach and Trailhead

Clermont

END

Western Trailhead

0   1/4   1/2
Mile

This is another short urban trail that will become part of a much larger network in the future. If you happen to be visiting the area, it's a nice trip along one of Florida's prettiest lakes. Take advantage of the swimming, fishing, and boating in the area. Clermont has become a major art center, and a visit "uptown" is worth the effort.

Created as two separate trails, the Clermont and Lake Minneola Scenic Trails share the same former rail line along Lake Minneola. The trail was built on the railroad bed of a CSX Transportation (formerly the Seaboard Coastline Railroad) line and was called the "Tug-n-Grunt" line by the local community. It mainly transported people and supplies for the turpentine industry—the mainstay of the area's economy before the pine trees were cut and the citrus trees extensively planted in the 1930s and 1940s. The rail-trail was built in 1998.

Though the ride from the east starts at the corner of Mohawk Road and Old Highway 50, the signs off US 27 that bring you to the trail will drop you off at the Minneola Trailhead, about 0.75 mile west of this intersection. Leave this trailhead and turn left to reach the Mohawk Road Trailhead.

Starting from Mohawk Road, the trail goes up and down a few hills through residential areas until it passes the Ed Harvey Shelter, 50 or 60 feet above the Minneola Trailhead.

From there it goes through a wooded area, with houses to your left and deep drops into the woods on unpaved trails to your right.

In a little over a mile, you'll pass under the double high bridges of US 27 into more densely developed areas, and start descending to Lake Minneola at mile 1.25. There are nice views of the lake from the top of the hill.

You reach the lake at mile 1.5; there the trail travels along the shore next to private homes until it reaches the public beach and picnic area, where you'll find rest rooms, a sandy beach, and parking. Along the lake you travel next to County Road 581. The trail has divided intersections at each road crossing—probably unnecessary, but someone's good idea.

At mile 2.0 the trail crosses the road and goes along the beach next to Bell's Ceramic factory. The public beach starts at mile 2.2,

The Lake Minneola shelter on the hillside above the Minneola Trailhead

with volleyball nets, rest rooms and picnic areas as well as water and public phones.

At mile 2.85 the trail goes through an elegant cement and brick promenade with railings, picnic tables, and a pier out into the lake. Just uphill from the promenade is a restaurant and dinner theater along with a bicycle shop. Farther up the hill is downtown Clermont.

The asphalt trail appears to end at the promenade, but you can continue until the trail turns into a cement sidewalk that takes you a short distance away from the lake and up a hill before resuming. From the lake to the trail's western termination you'll travel along the lakeshore, passing small cottages. The trailhead has parking, bathrooms, water, and phones.

One of the newer parts of the Nature Coast Greenway system, this trail circles the small town of Fanning Springs and gives access to one of the finest train trestles left in the state. The new planked surface with a widened viewing area provides a great place to watch for Suwannee River sturgeon, or just to relax above one of the nation's most famous rivers.

Activities:

Location: Gilchrist and Dixie Counties

Length: 4.0 miles

Surface: Asphalt; 12 feet wide

Wheelchair access: Throughout its length

Difficulty: Easy

Food: There is food available in the towns of Fanning Springs and Old Town at either end of the trail.

Rest room facilities: There are presently rest room facilities at Fanning Springs Recreation Area across the road, and at the small wayside park where US 19 crosses the Suwannee River. There will be some facilities at the Fanning Springs Trailhead in the future.

Seasons: Open all year.

Access and parking: You can access the trail along its length at various cross roads as well as the beginning and terminus of the trail. Both Fanning Springs and Old Town can be reached via Greyhound Bus connections if you want to chance it.

Rentals: Skates and bikes are available at the bike shop at the Fanning Springs Trailhead, open on weekends.

Contact: Manatee Springs State Park, 11650 Northwest 115th Street, Chiefland, FL 32626; (352) 493–6072.

• •

This pleasant little trail is located near a developing recreation hub where the Suwannee River is crossed by US 19 and US 98, and it gives a great view of typical Suwannee River floodplain habi-

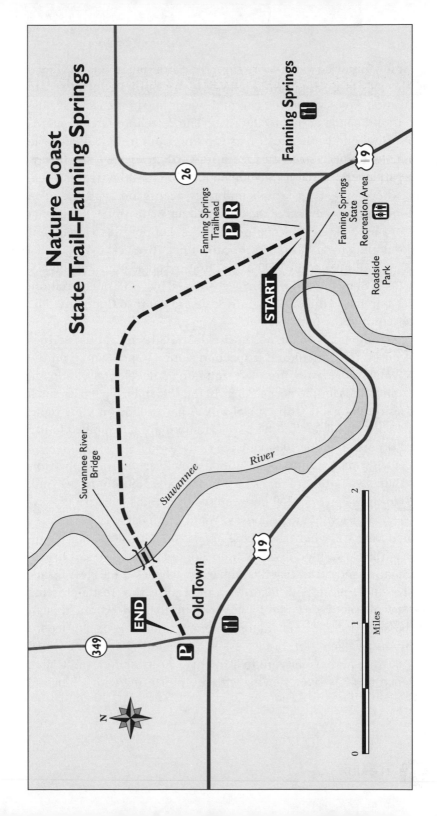

Nature Coast
State Trail–Fanning Springs

Fanning Springs

Fanning Springs Trailhead

P R

START

Fanning Springs State Recreation Area

Roadside Park

Suwannee River Bridge

END

Old Town

Suwannee River

P

349

26

19

19

N

0   1   2
Miles

tat. A few hundred yards away from the Fanning Springs Trailhead on the southern side of the highway is the Fanning Springs State Recreation Area, where you can find swimming in the clear spring-waters and canoe access to the river. The recreation area contains two springs and is the site of Fort Fanning, built in 1838 during the Seminole wars (no structures remain). Farther west is a small way-side park overlooking the Suwannee River. Across the river is a marina where large-boat rentals and river access are available. The Fanning Springs portion of the Nature Coast State Trail will become part of a much larger system in the future. For now, it's a small part of developing rural Florida in the Suwannee River valley.

This trail opened in 1999 as the first paved segment of the Nature Coast State Trail. It was formerly owned by CSX Transportation, which purchased the rail line from Seaboard Railroad Company. The state acquired the land in 1996.

The trailhead is on the northern side of US 19 in Fanning Springs adjacent to the agricultural inspection station. Once you're on the trail, you'll move away from the commercial development and follow utility lines for the next 4 miles. In the first mile you'll pass small houses on your left with typical mixed hardwoods on your right. Horses are prohibited on the paved trail but are encouraged to use the dirt portion of the 100-foot-wide right-of-way.

As with many rail-trails in Florida, you'll see active gopher tortoise burrows in the soft bank cuts or mounds adjacent to the trail. Look for these on your left between the trail and a local street serving a subdivision of small houses. You'll see most of these houses around mile 1.2, where the woods appear on both sides. As you approach the Suwannee River at mile 2.5, cross over a small bridge spanning a sandy draw that fills with water whenever the river floods.

The most prominent feature on the trail is the trestle crossing the Suwannee River at mile 3.3. It's been nicely planked, and though it's possibly a slight problem for skaters, it offers a good surface for bikers and walkers. The bridge is a large structure left in its original rust coating and visually quite attractive. At its center, the trail is widened to allow river viewing without interfering with other trail

The old train trestle

users. From here the trail is elevated across the river's floodplain, passing houses set up on pilings to escape the high flooding that can be common during wet periods, usually in the early spring. It reaches State Road 349 near the local airport, just north of Old Town where the pavement ends.

The Pinellas Trail is one of the best urban trails anywhere. It travels through the second most densely populated area in the country and yet retains rural characteristics in some of its segments. Paved from north of Tarpon Springs to the southern tip of the Pinellas Peninsula, there's never a moment when even the most jaded urbanite can't find junk food or a good view of the water. The challenging portions of this trail are the street crossings at heavy traffic periods, and the climbs up the overpasses, which require more effort than most rail-trails in Florida. The Pinellas County Planning Department has prepared a *Guide to the Pinellas Trail* that contains all you'll ever need to know about this trail. It's in its fourteenth printing, with more than 500,000 copies given away for free. It contains thirty-five pages of maps, food sources, and everything else you'd ever need to know to ride, skate, or walk this trail and have fun.

Activities:

Location: Pinellas County

Length: 35 miles

Surface: Asphalt; 12 to 14 feet wide

Wheelchair access: Throughout its length, though the overpasses may be too steep for some. If this could create a problem for you, check your route and wheel only those sections you'll feel comfortable on.

Difficulty: Easy

Food: It's everywhere in quantity and quality.

Rest room facilities: Numerous locations

Seasons: Open all year.

Access and parking: Numerous locations. Public transportation is available all along the trail.

Rentals: Skates, bikes, and bike trailers are available at various locations.

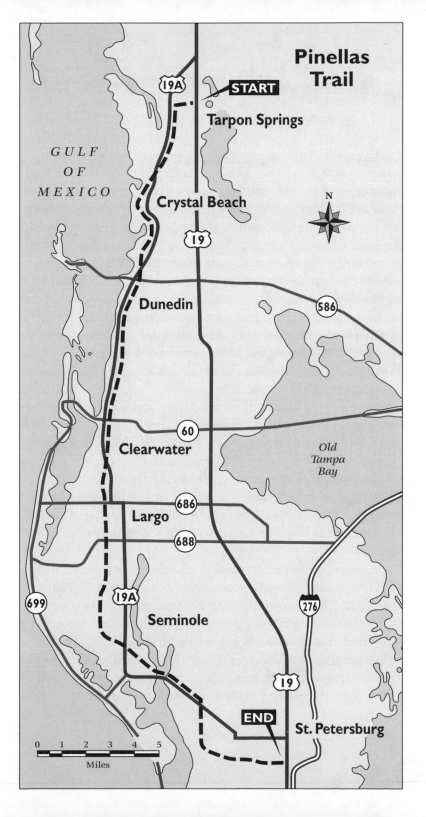

Pinellas
Trail

19A

START

Tarpon Springs

GULF
OF
MEXICO

Crystal Beach

N

19

586

Dunedin

60

Clearwater

Old
Tampa
Bay

686

Largo

688

699

19A

276

Seminole

19

END

St. Petersburg

0   1   2   3   4   5
Miles

Contact: The Pinellas County Planning Department, 14 South Ft. Harrison Avenue, Clearwater, FL 33756; (727) 464–4751. Mailing address: 315 Court Street, Clearwater, FL 33756.

• •

I f urban trails are what you're looking for, they don't come any better than this one. You can bicycle the Pinellas Trail in a single morning, or spend a week walking it with stops to explore all the towns along the way. You can take a side trip over to the beaches at Clearwater or to shop in downtown Dunedin. In some ways this trail epitomizes the definition of a linear park. As you approach each neighborhood, the activities increase, and hopscotch maps begin to appear chalked on the trail. At the main entrances to the subdivisions, you'll almost always see kids riding or lounging around the grassy edges watching you pass by as a possible intruder into their small sanctuary. There are plans to extend the northern portion of the trail around the peninsula to the east, and down south to a connection with the Gandy Bridge; this will take it over to Tampa, a distance of approximately 20 additional miles. From there the trail is expected to be extended to Bayfront Drive and ultimately up the Hillsborough River to Hillsborough River State Park.

More than 150 volunteer rangers patrol the trail for the county, and it would be rare indeed if you didn't pass a few of them in your travels. Stop and chat. They carry tales to take home with you.

Construction on this trail was started in 1990 on the previous Seaboard Coastline rail line. The present trail was completed in 1995, with the exception of the Cross Bayou Bridge, which was completed in 2000.

The trail's northern terminus is currently US 19 (mile 35.0) just north of Tarpon Springs (note that distances are measured from the southern terminus). It travels along the Anclote River for a mile before it takes a sharp bend into the city's urban area for another mile or so before pastureland starts appearing on the east.

At around mile 30.0 you pass under Harry Street, and the urban character starts reasserting itself. You can actually see the Gulf of Mexico to the west just before Ocean View Road at mile 29.0. From here the trail passes through the town of Crystal Beach at mile 28.0 on its way to downtown Palm Harbor at mile 27.0.

The trail crosses over Alt. US 19 at Orange Street on a nice overpass at mile 26.5, then leads you into various residential areas of the city of Dunedin at mile 22.5. Dunedin has all the amenities. From here the trail wanders through residential and commercial areas to the Stevenson Creek Bridge for a nice water view at mile 20.7. After the bridge come subdivisions and commercial and industrial areas north of the city of Clearwater. You hit the downtown area at mile 19.0.

South of Clearwater is commercial and light industrial for a mile; then residential areas predominate, with a few open parcels of land and some old orange groves. The overpasses at West Bay Drive at mile 15.5 and Ulmerton Road at mile 14.0 are steep and quite impressive. Watch out for the 20-mile-per-hour speed limit coming down and the strange terraced cement surfaces that can propel bicyclists and skaters into the air if they're not careful.

At mile 15.0 in a residential area of the town of Largo, you can take a spur to Taylor Park, which has a nice little reservoir and pic-

One of the tall road-crossing bridges on the Pinellas Trail

nic area. Continuing on the main trail, you pass through more residential areas before you reach the town of Seminole and Walsingham County Park at mile 13.0.

Downtown Seminole at mile 10.0 has full rest room and picnic facilities in the city park along with all the rest of the amenities you would look for on adjacent roads. Shortly after mile 8 you reach Cross Bayou and a bridge that was recently completed.

Just south of the trail on Boca Ciega Bay is War Veterans' County Park, with rest rooms, parking, and picnic and other facilities. South of Cross Bayou is an area filled with a big mall and other commercial establishments; by mile 6.0 residential areas once again predominate. From mile 5.0 to the trail's terminus at US 19 (Thirty-Fourth Street South in St. Petersburg), the trail passes a mix of commercial, industrial, and residential areas that are part of the city of St. Petersburg. The trail ends at Gibbs High School in the southern part of town.

Florida's first official state trail, the Tallahassee/St. Marks Historic Railroad Trail runs from the capital city to the coast on 19 miles of smooth pavement, passing a national forest and several small communities to end at the confluence of two beautiful rivers. Renowned as a workout ride for road bikers and skaters, it also leads to some fine off-road riding opportunities. And there are great opportunities for wildlife viewing with side visits into the Apalachicola National Forest or the St. Marks National Wildlife Refuge at the southern terminus. Start in Tallahassee and finish with a swim or a seafood dinner on the coast—or both.

Activities:

Location: Leon and Wakulla Counties

Length: 19 miles

Surface: The first 3.5 miles is asphalt 12 feet wide; the remainder is asphalt 8 feet wide

Wheelchair access: Throughout its length

Difficulty: Easy

Food: There are numerous gas and convenience stores at intersections after the first 2 miles, and you can find drinks and snacks at the concession at the main trailhead. The towns of Woodville and St. Marks contain various restaurants including Posey's, a local informal seafood landmark, 50 feet to your left at the trail's terminus.

Rest room facilities: There are rest rooms available at the main trailhead, the Woodville Sports Complex, and the Wakulla Station Trailhead. Convenience stores along the way also provide rest rooms for their customers.

Seasons: Open all year.

Access and parking: All along the trail's length at crossroads and trailheads. City transportation will get you as far as the main trailhead but no farther. Most buses have bike racks on the front. The concession at the main trailhead might be able to arrange a shuttle from the trailhead, but it's not an advertised service.

Rentals: Bikes, bike trailers, and skates can be rented at the main trailhead concession building.

Contact: Wakulla Springs State Park, 550 Wakulla Park Drive, Wakulla Springs, FL 32305; (850) 224–5950.

• •

T he Tallahassee/St. Marks Historic Railroad Trail gives you an exciting ride through history and a great opportunity to experience the unusual Florida transition between the urban present of Tallahassee and the rural past of the small fishing village of St. Marks. Though you can't totally get away from development that's taking place along the corridor, you'll pass by a section of the Apalachicola National Forest with good opportunities for wildlife viewing and end up across the river from the great salt-marsh vistas in the St. Marks National Wildlife Refuge. Add a visit to the Fort Apalachee de San Marcos Historic Site, and you'll ride from the present to 400 years into the past.

The trail was built in 1988 on the rail bed of the Tallahassee Railroad Company. The railroad was in turn constructed from Tallahassee to St. Marks in 1837 to transport cotton from farms in southern Georgia to the confluence of the St. Marks and Wakulla Rivers, 5 miles upriver from the Gulf of Mexico. A year later the railroad was extended 3 miles across the St. Marks River to Port Leon. When Port Leon was destroyed by a hurricane in 1843, the terminus was moved back to St. Marks, where it remained until the line was abandoned.

The railroad functioned initially as a mule-drawn cart system on wooden rails until 1856, when the wooden rails were replaced with steel and the first steam locomotives came into use. After the cotton bust of the early 1900s, the railroad transported mainly naval stores and wood products between Tallahassee and the coast. As the area began to urbanize and the naval supplies market gave way to modern petrochemicals, the use of the line steadily declined through the 1950s and 1960s until it was abandoned by its then owner, the Seaboard Airline Railroad, in 1983. The line was purchased by the Florida Department of Transportation and, with the use of legislative appropriations, was converted to a multiuse recreational trail.

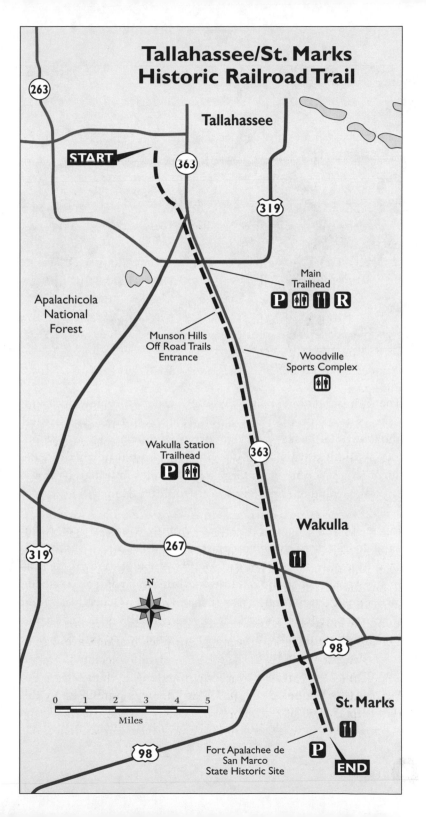

The main trailhead on the Tallahassee/St. Marks Trail

The trail is flat along its whole length except for a few occasional "rises" of no more than 5 or 6 feet. It starts in the urban area of southeastern Tallahassee, at the corner of Seaboard and Gamble Streets. While it travels mainly behind residential neighborhoods, it's surprisingly serene, with large oak canopies and high banks. It gives you a secluded experience you wouldn't expect in an urban setting.

In the fall you quickly get used to popping sounds as you travel over the acorns that litter many parts of the this portion of the trail. A few gray squirrels may compete with your feet, hooves, or tires for the acorns. Because the rail line was built in a rural area outside of town, construction around it was sparse until modern times, and most houses date back a way. After a mile you'll pass a small pond on your right, along with the only recognizable hill on the whole trail. It's actually 6 feet high.

The first 3.5 miles is a newer section managed by the city of Tallahassee and is asphalt, 12 feet wide. After about 3 miles the trail comes out of the canopy into a commercial and industrial area along State Road 363 (Woodville Highway), which it parallels for the next

2 miles until it connects with the main trailhead south of Capital Circle. (Mile 0.0 is painted on the trail here. Note that all of the mileages are measured from the main trailhead and are painted on each side of the trail at mile and kilometer intervals. They show cumulative total mileage on your right as you travel down and back.)

At the main trailhead management shifts from the city of Tallahassee to the Florida Park Service. The main trailhead has a parking lot, concession building, bathrooms, outdoor cold showers (hose), and historic markers and displays.

From the main trailhead the trail follows State Road 363 south. (It will eventually move a block or two away at mile 2.4 and come back again for a short stretch south of US 98 at mile 13.0.) Though the sounds of traffic on this road are blocked by trees when you move away from the road, it's always there as a reference and access to food and transportation.

Starting at the main trailhead is a sandy off-road bike and horse trail that follows the paved trail for the next 10 miles in relatively good shape, though the latter parts may a bit overgrown. (Access to the Munson Hills Off-Road Trail is also available from here but only over what is now private land. This stretch will hopefully be acquired soon by the park service.)

The first mile south of the main trailhead passes two small industrial parks and some woodlands before arriving at the Apalachicola National Forest and the official entrance to the Munson Hills Off-Road Trail at mile 1.3. There is a small paved rest area with water and a sandy single track leading to a pit toilet and display kiosk, which offers a trail map and information on local wildlife. This is a well-marked (blue blazes) 8-mile off-road trail with a 4-mile shortcut trail (white blazes) that's developed and maintained. It's suitable for all levels of recreationalists but can be very sandy in some places during extended dry periods.

Because the single track travels around small lakes and sinkholes through one of the country's more endangered habitats (longleaf pine and wiregrass), it's well worth the ride. Your chances of seeing an endangered red-cockaded woodpecker, Florida gopher tortoise, Sherman's fox squirrel, and various other wildlife species is good if you go early enough.

From the Munson Off-Road Trail cutoff, the paved trail passes the Woodville Recreation Complex at mile 2.3 with its playground, ball fields, and rest rooms. There are two emergency call boxes on the trail about miles 2.8 and 3.0 south of the complex. From here the trail crosses Oakridge Road at the beginning of the community of Woodville at mile 3.1. There are churches and houses along this part of the trail that thin out into a more rural setting around Bob Miller Road at mile 5.0. The rest of the trail to St. Marks continues with houses and trailers spread out along the way.

At about mile 8.7 is the new Wakulla Station Trailhead, with parking and rest rooms. At mile 9.8 the trail crosses Bloxham and Shadeville Roads in a split intersection. Take Bloxham Road to your right if you want to go to Wakulla Springs State Park, 4 miles to the west. This is a great place to eat, swim, or take a glass-bottomed boat ride over the clear waters of Wakulla Springs. A mile later on the trail, you come to a bench and water fountain provided by trailside homeowners, Robert and Amy Seidler.

At US 98 the trail passes the Primex Plant (ball gunpowder and explosives). Most of its buildings are near US 98 while the rest of its property along the trail is left in its natural state (pine and palmetto flatwoods). Some attempt has been made to restore the preexisting natural communities.

At the beginning of the town of St. Marks at mile 14.0, the houses become more numerous and the vegetation changes from pine upland to coastal hammock; cabbage palm trees and large hardwoods predominate. The present official end of the trail is at the riverfront in the town of St. Marks. Here you will find small restaurants serving local seafood, gift shops, and a small B&B just up the road.

In the future the trail will continue to your right to the Apalachee de San Marcos State Historic Site (0.5 mile) at the confluence of the St. Marks and Wakulla Rivers. For now you have to ride down public streets to get there. The fort has a small museum and some of the old walls from 400 years of occupation. You'll also find picnic tables along the river, a parking lot, a small beach, and a boat ramp for public use. It's a wonderful place to explore a little Florida history and jump in and cool off before you turn around and ride back.

16 West Orange Trail

The West Orange Trail passes through a mix of developing and rural Florida, a few miles west of metropolitan Orlando along the borders of Lake Apopka. Though the lake can only be seen in a few places, its influence is a major part of the history of the communities along this trail. At one time the most polluted lake in the state, Lake Apopka is making a comeback due to the efforts of the regional water management district and the state legislature. Once part of a thriving citrus industry, the area's growth and the suburban and urban connections to the trail have replaced most of the citrus trees except in a few areas around Winter Garden. This is Florida's only rail-trail that boasts a sign indicating that you are approaching a hill and need to use caution. The constant changes in scenery and the relaxed atmosphere of the towns along the way make this a great outing.

Activities:

Location: Orange County

Length: 19 miles

Surface: Asphalt; 14 feet wide

Wheelchair access: Throughout its length

Difficulty: Easy

Food: Each town along the way offers some food. The trail runs through the middle of Winter Garden, with numerous restaurants and food stores.

Rest room facilities: Available at County Line Station, Oakland Outpost, Winter Garden Station, Chapin Station, Ingram Outpost, Apopka-Vineland Outpost, and Clarcona Horseman's Park.

Seasons: Open all year.

Access and parking: County Line Station, Oakland Outpost, Winter Garden Station, Chapin Station, Ingram Outpost, Apopka-Vineland Outpost, and Clarcona Horseman's Park, as well as numerous cross roads along the way. There is public transportation from the Orlando area to various towns on the trail. Check with the Orange County Transportation Authority for up-to-date information.

Rentals: Bike and skate rentals are available at County Line Station and downtown Winter Garden.

Contact: Orange County Parks and Recreation Department, West Orange Trail, 455 East Plant Street, Winter Garden, FL; (407) 654–5150.

• • • • • • • • • • • • • • • • • • •

The West Orange Trail is 19 miles of the most interesting examples of changing Florida available in the state. The ride is sedate and the scenery ever changing. There are more large construction projects along this trail than any other. Massive expressway abutments are being built in a number of locations, as well as traffic bridges and exit ramps. New subdivisions are sprouting up in old orange groves, and small and large ranchettes are taking over cut-over woodlands on all sides. The trail even passes around three sides of a golf course with 20-foot fences to keep you from getting hit by golf balls. However, even with all these developments, this trail is a fun one. You're never far from a natural section of lake or woodland, and each new construction activity is more of a diversion than an intrusion. There are location markers at each mile and sometimes at 0.5-mile intervals on the side of the trail, so you should know where you are all the time. The trailheads are divided into

Passing Chapin Station through a grove of oak trees

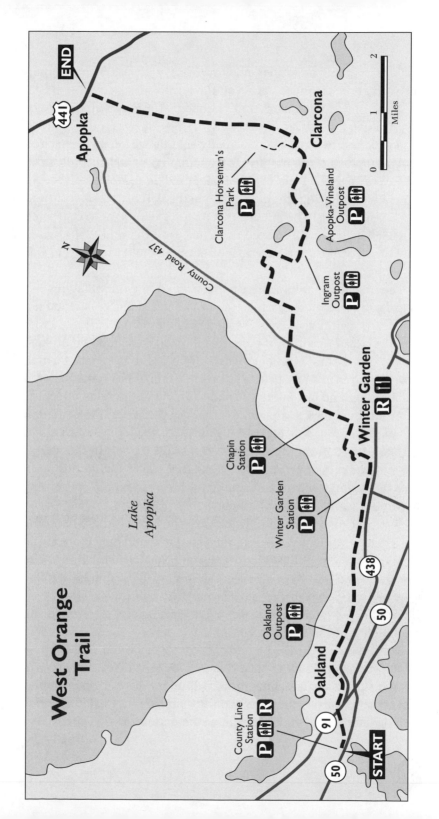

"stations" with full amenities, and "outposts" with less. The trail map provided at the trailheads gives all the locations.

Phase one of this paved trail opened in 1995, and phase two in 1998. Oakland, the first outpost north on the trail, was settled in 1844 as a citrus center. Fruit was originally sent by wagon to Tampa and then on to northern ports. In 1879 a shipping canal was built from Lake Apopka to the Dora chain of lakes and on to Welaka on the St. Johns River, allowing shipping between the Port of Jacksonville and East Coast markets. The rail line that the trail follows was constructed in 1886. The railroad replaced the canal until the mid-1950s, when trucks took over the major transportation role and the rail line was abandoned.

The trail leaves at its southern end from County Line Station with all its facilities, including a bike repair and rental place. The first notable feature after you leave the station is the railroad bridge across the Florida State Turnpike at mile 1.0. From there you proceed through mostly mixed rural orange groves and homes to Oakland, a small town settled in 1844 as a citrus center. The town has some restored old buildings and big oak trees (hence the name) to relax under.

Around mile 3.0 is a planted xeriscape garden and information sign just after Meadow Marsh. At mile 3.5 is one of only two views of Lake Apopka from the trail: You can see it way off in the west if you're traveling slowly. At mile 5.0 the trail reaches Winter Garden, once the center of citrus processing in the area and now becoming a bedroom community for Orlando.

The trail runs through the center of the town with landscaping and a road on either side. Restaurants, markets, and motels are found around the corner of East Plant Street and North Dillard Street. The newly restored Old Everglades Hotel is located in the middle of town; there are also two historical museums. The trailhead at Winter Garden Station, with bathrooms, water, parking, playground, and drink machines, is at the 5.1-mile mark.

From Winter Garden the trail travels north around some expensive developments sandwiched between orange groves and a few industrial sites. At mile 6.5 the only real hill on the trail shows up. A sign actually warns trail users about it—probably a good idea, since there is a crossroad and stop sign at the bottom. It isn't really that

The trail bridge on an old trestle over the Florida State Turnpike

steep, but when everything else is so flat, it does look impressive. About mile 6.0, the tree canopy closes in as you pass over a nice marsh system that feeds Lake Apopka.

Chapin Station at mile 7.0 has all the amenities of the other stations. It's recently built and will serve as a neighborhood park as well as a trailhead. It includes lots of playground equipment for the kids and an interesting bronze sculpture of a boy and girl on bikes.

Still going northeast you'll cross over a small stream and wetland on a wooden bridge next to a big pipeline at mile 8.0. In the summer it's a cooler area where you can catch your breath and smell and enjoy a real Florida swamp. From here you travel through some planted pines and more houses on your way to mile 8.5 and another quick view of Lake Apopka off to the west.

The next facility is Ingram Outpost at mile 12.0. The trail from Chapin Station to Ingram Outpost is a little more rural, except for the three-corner turn around the Forest Lake Golf Course of Ocoee. This section is also crossed several times by the Cross Town Expressway at mile 10.0; they look like standard road crossings, with big berms and bridges above you. The golf course has 20-foot-high chain-link fences all around it to keep you out and golf balls in. From mile 12.2 to 13.0 is a wooded section with good tree cover and mostly oak hammock vegetation. At mile 12.7 the trail crosses a nice small lake.

At mile 13.5 is the Apopka-Vineland Outpost, and a short distance beyond at mile 14.2 is the cutoff to Clarcona Horseman's Park. From there to mile 16.0 alternates nicely wooded sections with small ranchettes and lots of pretty horses. This is the most rural part of the trail and it continues with only a few breaks until you come to the outskirts of Apopka, where the trail becomes fully urban for the first time since downtown Winter Garden.

The wooded area just before Apopka, after Seventeenth Street, has a number of dirt trails that look interesting. These are probably local access trails for kids going to school or just places to ride for the locals, but they may be worth exploring.

At present the trail ends just south of US 441 in Apopka in the middle of a neighborhood of mixed houses and offices on Forest Drive. In the future it will extend 21 miles and include a connection to the Lake Minneola Scenic Trail to the west and Rock Springs Kelly Park to the north.

17 Withlacoochee State Trail

Currently, this is the longest existing paved rail-trail in Florida. It runs through an early-developed but still mostly rural part of the state from Citrus Springs (south of Dunnellon) in the north to Trilby (south of State Road 50) in the south. Its 46-mile length is entirely paved as it travels the Withlacoochee River valley through small towns, cattle ranches, wildlife management areas, and state forests. This trail will become part of the Central Florida Loop connection into the Cross Florida Greenway at Dunnellon sometime in the next five years. If you're serious about riding this trail purchase a copy of the *Withlacoochee State Trail Guide and Resource Book,* sold by the nonprofit support organization Rails to Trails of the Withlacoochee (P.O. Box 807, Inverness, FL 34451–0807; 352–726–2251).

Activities:

Location: Citrus, Hernando, and Pasco Counties

Length: 46 miles

Surface: Asphalt mixed with crushed rubber from recycled tires; 12 feet wide

Wheelchair access: Throughout its length

Difficulty: Easy

Food: There are food facilities at the junction of US 98/State Road 50 and I–75, near the Ridge Manor Trailhead, in every small town along the way, as well as at numerous locations on US 41 adjacent to the trail.

Rest room facilities: Rest room facilities are at every marked trailhead and all of the parks marked on the trail map. These include Citrus Springs, South Citrus Springs, Inverness, Ridge Manor, and Trilby Junction Trailheads. There are also rest rooms in the town parks along the way as well as the usual commercial establishments.

Seasons: Open all year.

Access and parking: There is parking at all the towns, trailheads, parks, and most crossroads shown on the map. A Greyhound bus can get you to the local towns, but don't count on any public transportation in between. Some of the bike rental places and the canoe livery may be willing to offer transport if you talk to them early.

Rentals: There is a bike and skate rental place north of Istachatta advertised on the trail and others in Inverness. You can also check in Floral City and Dunnellon. There are canoe liveries east of Nobleton on the Withlacoochee River.

Contact: Florida Park Service, 12549 State Park Drive, Clermont, FL 34711; (352) 394–2280.

• •

The Withlacoochee State Trail is the kind of rail-trail that lets you stretch out and enjoy a whole new world. Forget about schedules and annoying work hassles; this mostly flat trail will take you back into the historic Florida of the first real commercial era, when mining was king and people few and far between. You could ride this trail fast on a road bike in less than three hours, or you could take a leisurely three-day stroll and really enjoy it. What it lacks in topography, it makes up for in access to multiple recreational resources adjacent to or not far from the trail. The towns along the way have embraced the trail with the type of support that warms the heart, providing numerous places to shop, sleep, eat, fish, and swim. The camping in the Withlacoochee State Forest is excellent, and boating opportunities abound. Take time to ride the off-road trails in the Withlacoochee State Forest or canoe the Withlacoochee River at Nobleton. If you're a history buff, visit the restored downtown in Floral City.

The Withlacoochee River valley was one of the first areas mined for phosphate rock in Florida, because its rock was close to the surface and could be exported on the river for transshipment elsewhere. Present-day boaters on the Withlacoochee River can still see the deep holes and revegetated mounds from the mining industry that lasted into the early twentieth century before moving farther south. This lucrative market enticed the railroads into the area in the late 1800s. By 1885 Henry Plant had extended his railroad north through Dade City and Trilby to Croom. In 1891 the Silver Springs, Ocala and Gulf Railroad Company line was extended southwestward from Silver Springs to Dunnellon and through Hernando to Inverness. In 1893

the line from Croom was extended north through Floral City to Inverness to connect the whole route. This system eventually became the Atlantic Coast Line Railroad in 1902, which was changed to the Seaboard Coast Line in 1967, and CSX Transportation in 1980. The line was purchased from CSX by the state in 1989, and paving starting in 1992. Today the trail is completely paved for all 46 miles. It was one of the earlier corridors purchased for trail use in Florida.

You can ride the trail from either direction, so our advice is to determine the predominant winds on ride day and go with them. Mile markers are painted on brown plastic posts that look like steel rails. There are numerous places where horses cross the trail, but they are otherwise kept pretty much on dirt adjacent to it throughout its length.

The present southern terminus of the trail is a small path that leads out to US 301/US 98, 5 miles south of State Road 50 on the northern side of the highway. It's not marked, so it's easy to miss if you don't look carefully. If you cut in on State Road 575 to Trilby, there are directional signs that will help.

As you leave from the south, the trail passes through the small community of Trilby before the houses thin out into small and large cattle ranches intermixed with rural homes. At about mile 5.0, the trail comes close to the Withlacoochee River with its floodplain vegetation and a large Wal-Mart distribution center. From there it crosses over US 98/State Road 50 on a very impressive old train trestle into the Ridge Manor Trailhead at mile 6.0. This is a full-facility trailhead and is often used as the southern trail terminus.

From Ridge Manor, the trail passes mixed wooded areas with various-sized cattle ranches. The trail is either elevated or cuts through the hills, maintaining its elevation with only slight changes. A few miles from Ridge Manor, you can see lots of gopher tortoise burrows in soft sand mounds with an occasional tortoise munching grass along the edges of the trail. As with most Florida trails, there are a lot of fire ant mounds along the edges. Avoid these if you go off the trail for any reason.

At mile 8.0 the trail crosses over Croom-Rital Road and continues into the Withlacoochee State Forest with its planted pines and mixed hardwoods. A little past mile 11.0 the trail crosses under I–75.

From here the Withlacoochee State Forest Croom Motorcycle Area starts on your left, though the riding trails are not obvious from the trail.

At mile 12.0 the trail crosses the Croom-Rital Road again to come closer to the Withlacoochee River. The area through the forest has a few more small sandy hills than other parts of the trail, with pine and mixed oaks on both sides except near the river, where hardwood floodplain vegetation comes close to the trail. Unfortunately, the river is not visible from the trail, though if you're riding an off-road bike you might consider some side trips here.

You leave the forest at mile 14.5 when you cross Edgewater Avenue (marked on a small sign attached to the impressive trail gates at road crossings). Lake Townsen Park starts on your right at mile 15.0 just across Lake Lindsey Road (County Road 476), but the main facilities are to your left a few hundred feet farther on.

The park has mowed areas down to the trail and provides rest rooms, picnic tables, a fishing pier, and ball fields. It also fronts on

The Floral City trailhead rest stop at the site of the old railroad terminal

A gopher tortoise munching on trailside grass

the Withlacoochee River to your right of the trail. Some of the crushed rubber that went into the asphalt to build the trail is laid on the parking area roads. It's a weird surface to travel on.

If you turn right onto County Road 476, you can head into the town of Nobleton to take advantage of canoe rentals at the bridge that crosses the Withlacoochee River, 0.25 mile away. There is also limited food here.

At mile 16.2 you pass through the town of Istachatta, supposedly the site where Hernando de Soto crossed the Withlacoochee River in 1539. Hampton's Bike Shop is here, with a number of rentals available. Outside Istachatta there are large cattle ranches with some trailers mixed in on both sides. The trail generally follows County Road 39, crossing over in various places.

Just past mile 23.0, the trail crosses County Road 48 next to US 41 in Floral City. Here you'll find food, gas, and small gift shops. There is a sign pointing right to the Historic District. At the intersection is the Floral City Trailhead, with rest rooms, water, a picnic area, and a small covered gazebo. A pleasant little place, this is the location of the former train depot built in 1893 at the height of phosphate mining in the area. During that time the city reached a population of 10,000 people, one of the largest cities in Florida.

To your right at mile 27.0 starts Fort Cooper State Park; you can reach the entrance if you turn right onto Fort Cooper Road then left onto Old Floral City Road (about 3 miles). Swimming, camping, picnicking, and nature trails are available. The park was named for Maj. Mark Anthony Cooper, commander of five companies of the First Georgia Volunteers during the Second Seminole War (1836).

After you pass the park property at mile 27.0, the houses on your left become more numerous as you approach the town of Inverness during the next 3 miles. At mile 30.5 you reach Wallace Brooks Park, with parking, swimming, picnicking, and rest rooms. From there you're only a few hundred yards from downtown Inverness, with plenty of food and other amenities.

At mile 31.2 you pass under the Henderson Trestle where US 41 crosses; proceed adjacent to the highway for the next 13 miles. This section is the most highly developed area of the trail, with convenience stores, shopping areas, and houses on both sides.

At mile 35.0 is the town of Hernando; Hernando Beach County Park is on your left across US 41. Turn right at Lake Place to reach the park.

From Hernando the trail passes a mixed rural area with some farmlands, pinewoods, and small homes. The South Citrus Springs Trailhead is at mile 41.5. It has parking, water, and rest rooms. From here the trail continues along US 41 for a while until its present terminus at Citrus Springs and Haitian Avenue. Rest rooms, parking, and a picnic area are developed at this trailhead.

In the future the trail will be continued into the town of Dunnellon where it will connect to the Cross Florida Greenway hub. All in all, a fine outing from beginning to end.

MORE RAIL-TRAILS

I n a number of places around the state are rail-trails that for one reason or another don't measure up to the criteria for "Florida's Top Rail-Trails." It's not that they aren't pleasant places to spend some time; we simply needed to make some decisions because of space limitations. All of the following trails are passable to some extent, though their level of day-to-day maintenance may be suspect. Future editions of this book may upgrade some of these trails to "Top" status if more segments are completed, they become safer to use, or they're connected to other trails. For now, consider these trails a little more of an adventure than the others and use them accordingly.

18 Bell Trail

Gilchrist County, 0.8 miles. This small grass and dirt trail in Bell, 30 miles west of Gainesville, is used mostly by local residents for short walks.

19 Florida Keys Overseas Heritage Trail

The sections listed below are part of a 120-mile trail that will run the length of the entire Florida Keys along the route of the old Henry Flagler railroad. It will use many of the old bridges as well as new, raised travelway connectors. Most of the trail is over or along water with spectacular views of the Florida Keys. Each section will feature access to attractions, food, lodging, and shopping along the way. When completed, it will become one of the premier rail-trails in the country. At the time of publication, seven sections of this trail are mostly complete, and the total project is in the planning and funding stage. Note that these trails often begin or end at roadways or bridges that have inadequate room for trail users, causing potentially dangerous interactions with heavy traffic.

- Channel 5 Section. 1.0 miles; asphalt; mile markers 12–13
- Cudjoe Key Section. 2.0 miles; dirt; mile markers 20.5–23.0

- Bahia Honda to Little Duck Key. 3.0 miles; asphalt; mile markers 37–40
- Marathon Key to Pidgeon Key Section. 2.3 miles; asphalt; mile markers 45–47
- Tom's Harbor Section. 5.0 miles; asphalt and dirt; mile markers 51.5 59.5
- Long Key to Conch Key. 2.3 miles; asphalt; mile markers 65.0–68.5
- Lower Matacombe Section. 4.4 miles; asphalt; mile markers 74–77

20 Fakahatchee Strand State Preserve Trails

These trails travel along old tram dikes used in the nineteenth and early twentieth centuries mainly for transporting logs out of the Big Cypress Swamp (now the Big Cypress National Preserve). They run through the interesting Everglades communities of southern Florida and past miles of sawgrass, pine flatwoods, cypress swamps, and the largest royal palm hammock left in the state. These trails should probably be considered more park trails than rail-trails, but because they do use former rail beds (even though quite temporary), we've included them here. (Contact: P.O. Box 548, Copeland, FL 33926; 941–695–4593).

- Jones Grade Trail. 6.0 miles; grass surface; Collier County
- Mud Tram Trail. 1.0 miles; grass surface; Collier County
- South Main Trail. 3.0 miles; grass surface; Collier County
- West Main Trail. 3.0 miles; grass surface; Collier County

21 Flagler Trail

Seminole County. 13 miles; gravel and grass surface. This is a trail slated for future construction on the bed of the old Flagler Railroad. No completion date has been set, and only small portions are passable at present. (Contact: Seminole County Parks and Recreation, 264 West North Street, Altamonte Springs, FL 32714; 407–788–0405).

22 Stadium Drive Bikepath

Leon County. 1.5 miles; paved. This trail is a student transportation bike path on the Florida State University campus built on an abandoned rail corridor. It may one day be connected to the Tallahassee/

St. Marks Historic Railroad State. (Contact: City of Tallahassee, Traffic Engineering Division, 300 South Adams, Tallahassee, FL 32301–4555; 850–922–6007).

23 Upper Tampa Bay Trail

Hillsborough County, Citrus Springs. 3.0 miles; paved. This very new trail was finished too late for inclusion in "Florida's Top Rail-Trails." (Contact: Hillsborough County Parks and Recreation Department, 7508 Ehrlich Road, Tampa, FL 33625; 813–264–8511.)

THE FLORIDA TRAIL SYSTEM

T he individual trails described in this book are all part of the Florida Trail System. Though each individually is a good destination to ride or explore on foot, together they form the beginning of a system that will enhance their usefulness as a major recreational resource for the citizens of the state as well as our millions of visitors each year.

The basis for this system is the "hub, node, point, and connector" concept of trail development. Though these terms are best described in the context of a specific location, they each have an importance in a system that should be easily understandable. A hub is a major center for multiuse trails that are general destinations for a large area. A node is a specific destination for trails that could be part of a hub, but is usually used only as a single-day outing combined with other recreational pursuits, often at a state or regional park. A point is a place of interest that doesn't necessarily contain multiuse recreational trails; it's a stop along a trail or a destination that trail users might seek out for historic or other recreational benefits. A connector is a trail that links hubs, nodes, and points, such as a rail-trail.

Florida has three hubs that in the future will become the backbone of the system. Each hub has trails that are currently used to some extent but are continuously being upgraded and improved. This chapter will describe the hubs in this system and their present and projected future trail usage as part of the Florida system.

Remember, this is a dynamic trail system that is changing all the time. Additions and improvements have been made since this book was published, and many more will be made in the future. Contact the Office of Greenways and Trails (Florida Department of Environmental Protection, Douglas Building, 3900 Commonwealth Boulevard, Tallahassee, FL 32399–3000) or check the DEP Web site for the latest information.

Though it may seem logical to start at one end of the state and describe each hub in sequence, because the Cross Florida Greenway is the most developed at this time, I have decided to start in the middle and work out in each direction.

The Cross Florida Greenway (CFG) was created from the dying remnants of a federal public works project called the Cross Florida Barge Canal. This project was initiated in the late 1930s as a means of allowing ships to travel through the Florida peninsula without having to go far to the south into dangerous waters patrolled by German submarines in the pre–World War II days. It started with some minor construction at its western end, but otherwise things never really got off the ground.

Because of the United States' entry into the war in 1941, work was delayed until President Lyndon Johnson got it started again in the early 1960s. However, by late in that decade a number of Gainesville professors at the University of Florida, led by Marjorie and Archie Carr, realized the negative environmental impact this project would have and used it to rally Florida's awakening environmental movement.

Faced with numerous lawsuits and a tight federal budget, President Nixon halted construction in 1971. From that time until 1991, the future of the canal remained in limbo until Congress deauthorized the project, the first deauthorization of a public works project in U.S. history. The 120 miles, encompassing more than 77,000 acres, is now officially the Marjorie Harris Carr Cross Florida Greenway, a multiuse recreational area offering boating, fishing, swimming, hiking, horseback riding, bike riding, and hunting.

Because the CFG runs from Palatka on the St. Johns River to the east, and Yankeetown on the Gulf of Mexico to the west, it is a logical hub for the central Florida area.

There are presently numerous multiuse trails in the CFG, as well as plans to connect them so that you will be able to travel from one end to the other without needing to use public roads. One of the most imposing features is a land bridge over I–75 near Belleview that will be completed in 2000. This is the first land bridge built over an interstate in the United States. (The bridge appears to be a standard expressway overpass when viewed from below. However, the top is covered with soil and native vegetation to look like part of the adjacent forest. The off-road trail meanders across it.)

Within the CFG corridor are substantial boating opportunities on the wide canal in the west, on the Withlacoochee and Oklawaha Rivers, as well as on the whole St. Johns River system that connects with the Oklawaha River in the east. There are designated canoe trails as well as landings and campgrounds.

The Ocala National Forest adjoins the CFG in the eastern reaches where trails will connect into the Florida system. The Florida National Historic Trail (hiking-only over much of its length) crosses the greenway near the eastern terminus. This trail will ultimately run from Pensacola to Miami.

Santos Trailhead

For the next few years, the trailhead at Santos (midway between Ocala and Belleview, just off US 441) will be the main focus of trail riding in the CFG. This area has some of the best-established and -maintained off-road riding trails in the state. A project of the Ocala Mountain Bike Association, a private nonprofit organization, these trails are suitable for all levels of riders.

If you start at the Santos Trailhead, you will find a map that describes all of the trails and indicates their level of difficulty. Yellow trails are the easiest; blue trails have a few rocks and roots; red trails are top-grade technical trails for the advanced rider that go in and out of a series of limerock pits. Yellow and blue trails are suitable for any level of rider, though new riders may want to walk a few parts of the blue trails.

Because many of the trails crisscross each other within a fairly confined area, it's not hard to get confused, but it's difficult to get totally lost. If you just keep going, you'll end up someplace familiar.

The longest ride on a single trail (without confusing cross trails) is out to I–75 on the Poison Spider section of the trails. These trails are all on twisty dirt single track in the woods and cover around 25 miles out and back. In the future this section will cross over the new land bridge; continue to the Dunnellon area alongside the Withlacoochee River; and end up in Yankeetown as part of the Cross Florida Off-Road Trail.

A number of horse trails also start at Santos. If you're riding a bike, stay away from these. The surface is too chewed up for fun riding.

Here are some of the recreational opportunities that this hub offers:

- Yankeetown, Gulf of Mexico—boating, salt- and freshwater fishing
- Withlacoochee River and Lake Rousseau—boating, freshwater fishing, swimming, hiking, nature observation, model airplane flying
- Santos Trailhead—off-road bicycle and horseback riding
- Marshal Swamp Trailhead—nature trail, historic Civil War site
- Marion County Urban Greenway—sports complex, ball fields, hiking, horseback and bike riding
- Oklawaha River—boating, fishing, swimming, camping
- Rodman Reservoir—fishing, camping, Florida National Scenic Trail (hiking-only)
- Buckman Lock—St. John's River Loop trails for hiking, horses
- St. John's River—boating, fishing

B Lake Okeechobee Trail Hub

Lake Okeechobee is the largest freshwater lake that's wholly contained within the U.S. land mass. It's the "plumbing center" of southern Florida, collecting rainwater from the central part of the state and discharging it to the ocean on the east and west coasts; to the adjacent sugar, citrus, and vegetable farms; and, ultimately, to Everglades National Park at the southern end of the peninsula. The lake was diked by the U.S. Army Corps of Engineers in another of those ill-conceived water projects of the first half of the twentieth century. Once the $33 million project is complete, the Lake Okeechobee Trail Hub will become south Florida's major recreational trail destination.

Though the lake is a magnificent body of water in scope and grandeur, it suffers from all the environmental insults you would expect from a system managed with too many goals and too little understanding of the natural system it serves. From excess nutrients pouring into the lake (causing substantial algal blooms), to disruptions of natural fresh- and saltwater interactions when excess water is released to the coasts, to hydro-period interference in the Everglades, this system is an expensive mess.

No one thinks the money spent on constructing trails around the lake will solve any of the environmental problems, but who cares? The trail will be great, and this part of the Florida Trail System will attract many users once it's finished.

Though an unpaved trail (of sorts) presently exists along the dike, few people want to experience the punishment of the poor surfaces (gravel and clumps of grass) and lack of shelter that it currently presents. The plans call for a paved 120-mile trail mainly along the top of the Lake Okeechobee dike system through six Florida counties. Shelters, benches, water, and rest rooms will be built to complement the recreation facilities that already exist in the area. This trail is scheduled for completion by 2005. A detailed plan for the trail can be obtained from the Office of Greenways and Trails (Florida Department of Environmental Protection, Douglas Building, 3900 Commonwealth Boulevard, Tallahassee, FL 32399–3000; 850–488–3701).

The following are the public recreational amenities in the area that will eventually be connected by the trail. You can use them now if you want to ride the lake dike or adjacent paved roads. Most have rest rooms and water, but I suggest checking before making a trip to the area if you will depend on them for a long trip.

- Clewiston Recreation Area
- Alvin Ward Senior Park
- Moorhaven Recreation Village
- Fisheating Creek Recreation Area
- Harney Pond Recreation Area
- Big Bear Beach Recreation Area
- Indian Prairie Recreation Area
- Buckhead Ridge Recreation Area
- Okee-Tantie Recreation Area
- C. Scott Driver Junior Park
- Okeechobee Beach Park
- Nubbin Slough Recreation Area
- Henry Creek Recreation Area
- Chancey Bay Recreation Area
- Port Mayaka Recreation Area
- Canal Point Recreation Area
- Pahokee State Park
- Bacom Point Recreation Area
- Paul Rardin Park
- Belle Glade Recreation Area
- John Stretch Park

There is no prettier place in northern Florida than the Suwannee River valley, with its black-water rivers and clear-flowing springs. Here you'll find banks covered with tall pines and hardwoods, some with wide riding trails and others with twisty single tracks. Though there is extensive mining in some areas, the most scenic lands have been preserved in a unique partnership between various governmental and private enterprises.

The anchors for the hub are three units of the state park system within 25 miles of each other. These parks are connected by parcels owned and managed by the Suwannee River Water Management District, the Florida Fish and Wildlife Commission, and the Florida Division of Forestry. A few miles to the east of the hub is the Osceola National Forest, which connects to the Okefenokee Swamp National Wildlife Refuge and Forest in Georgia.

The recreational opportunities in the area are without peer. Though canoeing the 184 miles of the Suwannee River tends to get the most attention, miles of easy to intermediate off-road trails abound. Each year the Suwannee Bicycle Association holds its Iditeride on 50 miles of the best trails in the White Springs area—only a small portion of what's available.

The river and the trails give access to more than a hundred clear springs of different sizes and shapes, many of which are available for swimming and diving. The small towns along the way are beginning to understand the economic potential of eco-tourism and visitors interested in outdoor recreation. For example, spring-to-spring tours by boat and bike are now being offered in some locations.

The Suwannee hub will be connected by a number of trails planned for the future. The present rail-trail from Jacksonville that now ends in Baldwin (see Trail 11) may be continued farther west to connect with trails into the hub. The most recently purchased rail corridor runs from Palatka in the southeastern section and will connect to Lake City, due south of White Springs, a distance of more than 65 miles (the Palatka/Lake Butler/Lake City Rail Trail.) In the western section of the hub, you can eventually expect to see trails from as far south as Cedar Key on the Gulf of Mexico join with trails from Chiefland and Manatee Springs to Fanning Springs along the Nature Coast Trail (see Trail 13) to Branford, Live Oak, and Suwannee River State Park. These will then be connected to trails going as far west as Pensacola.

A note of caution for all the Suwannee River trails: The Suwannee floods often and heavily, usually between January and April. When the water is high, many of the trails and springs are under water. Always check water levels beforehand by calling one of the parks. Even canoeing can become dangerous in high flood, and campsites along the river may be limited.

Suwannee River State Park (Route 8, Box 297, Live Oak, FL 32060; 904–362–2746) – Located at the confluence of the Withlacoochee (running south from Georgia—not to be confused with the river of the same name in the west-central part of the state) and Suwannee Rivers at the western end of the hub, this 1,800-acre park is a prime swimming, camping, and boating location. Leave I–10 at exit 39 west of Live Oak and drive 5 miles north.

Though bicycles and horses are not permitted on trails in this park, numerous connectors exist outside the park for those who choose to use this park for camping. There are flowing springs on the riverbank, lots of opportunities to fish and boat, and Civil War earthworks to explore.

Stephen Foster State Folk Cultural Center (P.O. Drawer G, White Springs, FL 32096; 904–397–4331) – Built to memorialize Stephen Collins Foster and his song of the Suwannee River, "Old Folks at Home," this 247-acre music and folk center is also home to some pleasant trails that wind around the Carillon Tower and campground. In the center of the White Springs trail area, this park provides extensive camping, boating, swimming, and arts and crafts, along with various music and crafts festivals during the year. When its new cabins are finished in 2001, this will become one of the best places to camp when you're riding the trails of the area.

Big/Little Shoals State Park (Suwannee River Water Management District, Route 3, Box 64, Live Oak, FL 32060; 904–362–1001) – On the eastern side of the hub, this new state park and recreation area (next to the only two rapids of any size on the Suwannee River) is presently under construction. Though the park is presently planned for only the Little Shoals area, negotiations have gone back and forth with the water management district to create some connection with the Big Shoals Recreation Area upstream. Because the future is uncertain, and the trails will probably be available regardless of the status of the land management, we've included both areas as part of the park and referred to them as a single park here for convenience.

Big/Little Shoals State Park has numerous multiuse trails as well as a launching area for canoe trips into White Springs that will land you at the Stephen Foster Folk Cultural Center if you wish. There are both double- and single-track trails, with maps available at the park office or from the Suwannee Bicycle Association office in White Springs. The lands adjoin wildlife management areas that are still hunted from time to time, so be prepared to wear bright colors or go somewhere else for hunting season.

The following are trails listed from the western end of the hub near Suwannee River State Park and ending at Big/Little Shoals State Park:

- Twin Rivers (8 miles)
- Holton Creek (16 miles)
- Mattair Spring (11 miles)
- Camp Branch (6 miles)
- Carter Camp (6 miles)
- Bridge to Bridge (5 miles)
- Gar Pond (6 miles)
- Little Shoals (2.5 miles)
- Big Shoals (18 miles)

Florida's

• • • • • • • • • • • • • • • • • •

TOP STATE PARK
TRAILS

The trails described in this chapter embody some of the unbelievable beauty and majesty of the Florida Park System—voted the best in the United States for 1999–2000. They also point up some of the problems associated with park trails and the new attitudes that are shaping up to make improvements in the future.

Most of the 152 units of the Florida Park System have some riding opportunities, even if they're just a few hundred yards of paved driveway. However, only a few can presently be classified as good trail systems that will attract serious riders, or even beginners looking for a sustained and pleasant riding experience. We understand that because of a new awareness and commitment from the park service, this situation will improve over the next few years. For now, be happy with the twelve units that presently have the trails that are featured below.

Lands managed by the Florida Park Service include parks, historic monuments, gardens, recreation areas, cultural centers, preserves, reserves, and trails. For the purposes of this book, they will be referred to as either trails or parks. State-managed rail-trails are included in the rail-trail section of this book. We'll refer to all of the others as parks even if they happen to be officially called something else.

As with most state park systems in the country, the major goals of the Florida Park System are to protect the state's beautiful, endangered, and unusual natural resources as well as to provide nondestructive recreational activities compatible with resource protection. It's only been in the last part of the twentieth century that Florida parks have increased emphasis on the recreational user and acquired land that is particularly suited for recreational purposes.

Unfortunately, building multiuse trails suitable for bicycles has not been a top priority in the past. Now, however, with the increase in bicycling activities throughout the country, more and more parks have begun to open up their systems to bicycle use. Because we are at the beginning of this movement, a number of problems are showing up; they should be resolved in the next few years.

First, few of the parks have consistent signage. This means that finding trailheads and understanding where you are on a particular trail may be difficult until you become familiar with that trail. Second, there are no standards for degrees of difficulty. Though most trails are for beginners, parts of others are more challenging, and you may not find this out until you're 3 or 4 miles from the start. User conflicts have not been well thought out in some parks. Many of the trails that permit bikes also allow horses. This works fine in some parks, but not in others whose surfaces have been churned to deep sand or washboards. Some trails are built by knowledgeable local bike clubs, others by park personnel with little or no bicycling experience. Some parks list their sandy firebreaks as bicycle trails while others use wonderful enclosed canopy woodlands.

If you intend to travel to a specific park to ride its trails, and you don't see it listed in this book, I would suggest calling ahead for a good description of what you'll be riding. Call for camping reservations as well. All parks take reservations well in advance, and camping spaces are often filled on weekends. All of the rest room and parking facilities in the parks are suitable for the handicapped. Paved trails are available for skaters as well as bikes unless marked otherwise.

Enjoy the trails that are there today and be ready to return for the trails coming tomorrow.

Fort Clinch State Park

Surrounded by water on three sides, this narrow peninsula park in the northeastern corner of Florida is a marvelous natural and historic site with all amenities open to the casual rider. Its paved and unpaved riding is outstanding.

Activities:

Location: Nassau County

Trails: Paved or stabilized 3.5 miles; unpaved 6.5 miles

Food: Available at Fernandina Beach near the park entrance

Lodging and Camping: There are twenty-one campsites on the beach and forty-one in the coastal oak hammock near the river. Both areas have rest rooms, showers, laundry, phones, and electrical and water hookups. The beach campsites are in an open field with no shade. There are numerous motels in Fernandina Beach and other places on Amelia Island.

Contact: Fort Clinch State Park, 2601 Atlantic Avenue, Fernandina Beach, FL 32034; (904) 277-7274.

• •

This park was established around Fort Clinch, a fort built by the U.S. government during the Seminole wars that was also used by both Confederate and Union forces in the Civil War. It was briefly recommissioned for the Spanish American War and World War II. Purchased by the state in 1935 (256 acres), it was opened to the public in 1938. The bike trails were added in the late 1990s.

The bike trails at Fort Clinch offer the second best park riding trails for serious riders in the Florida Park System. Enjoy them before you take a quick swim in the ocean, enjoy a leisurely walk in the woods, or explore the old fort.

A note of caution. Signs that contain the no-bicycle emblem (a bicycle with red circle and line through it) don't mean "no bicycles." They're simply the park's way of telling you that the trails are designed in a one-way system (counterclockwise), and you shouldn't enter at that point. It's obvious once you figure out the pattern. In

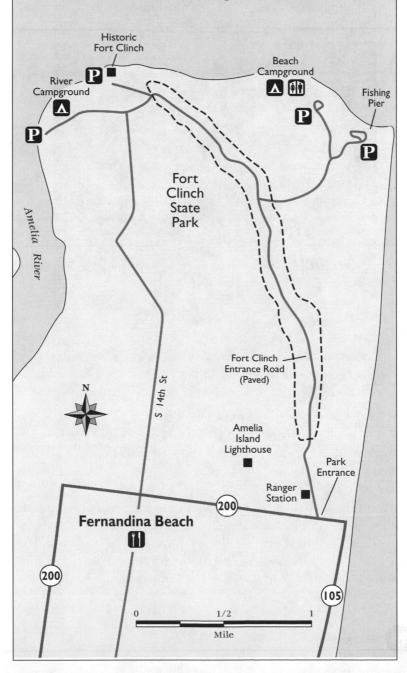

Fort Clinch
State Park

St Marys Entrance

Historic
Fort Clinch

River
Campground

P

Beach
Campground

Fishing
Pier

P

P

Fort
Clinch
State
Park

Amelia River

N

Fort Clinch
Entrance Road
(Paved)

S 14th St

Amelia
Island
Lighthouse

Park
Entrance

Ranger
Station

200

Fernandina Beach

200

105

0   1/2   1
Mile

The author starting out at Fort Clinch Trail

addition, because the single track emerges onto the paved road periodically to offer rest areas and give you the option of returning on the park road, it often appears that the trail ends before it actually does. If you're in doubt, look to your right and you'll see any continuations.

The entrance road leads to the Seminole war fort, campgrounds, beaches, and fishing pier. It's 3.5 miles of easy riding and good scenery. The wide asphalt road travels through the coastal hammock and between the main dune system and the ocean (except for a few hundred yards of limerock in the riverside campground).

The unpaved bike trail is another matter. This narrow single track will please even the most experienced riders. Rank novices may not want to try it, but beginners with some experience can have a lot of fun if they're willing to walk a few hills. It's a rare opportunity to ride a natural system in a park on trails designed and built by bike riders.

This trail officially starts at the fort parking lot. Rapidly climb a 15-foot-tall dune, then off you go down into a twisty, rooty single track that stays within 100 yards of either side of the main entrance park road. The trail goes up, down, and around, then back up and down throughout its whole length, out and back. The ups are high enough that all but the strongest riders will have to stand, and the downs are steep enough to get you way back and behind your saddle if you want to stay upright. On the return trip you'll have to ride for a few hundred feet on the paved road in a spot where the off-road trail would have damaged some large sandy dunes.

During dry periods some parts of the trail become very sandy and difficult as you approach the tops of the big dunes. The rest is fine, however, except for the occasional mud hole that hasn't dried up. During rainy periods there will be lots of muddy places, but the sandy spots will be packed down and nice to ride. Conditions will be best a few days after a light soaking rain.

This off-road trail is worth making a special trip to ride.

2   Guana River State Park

Guana River State Park is mainly a beach park with some very nice riding areas hidden away in a coastal hammock at its southeastern end. Only a few miles from St. Augustine, the park provides great Atlantic Ocean swimming and surf fishing as well as some freshwater lake fishing. The bicycle trails are thoroughly delightful and would be enjoyed by all levels of riders and hikers. The absence of horses and existence of the tree canopy allows the unpaved road surfaces to be maintained in reasonable shape for bikes. Lots of rain will result in some mud holes, but most areas should be navigable.

Activities:

Location: St. Johns County

Trails: Dirt double track, 8.5-plus miles

Food : Available at South Ponte Vendra Beach on US A1A.

Lodging and Camping: There is no camping in the park. You'll find motels in Villano Beach and St. Augustine.

Contact: Guana River State Park, 2690 South Ponte Vendra Boulevard, Ponte Vendra Beach, FL 32082.

• • • • • • • • • • • • • • • • • • •

Guana River State Park is a recent acquisition for Florida (1980s). It's composed of 2,400 acres that include not only the trails but also substantial beachfront on the Atlantic Ocean. There is physical evidence of Native American occupation dating as far back as 5,000 years ago, with some historic evidence that Ponce de Leon may have landed here in his first expedition to Florida. In the 1600s, the Spanish established a mission here on the Tolomato River, but no physical evidence of structures has been found.

If you combine this park's trails with the water management district trails to the north, a good day's riding can result. Be aware that hunting is allowed on the water management lands during parts of the year. Do not be confused by this park's multiple en-

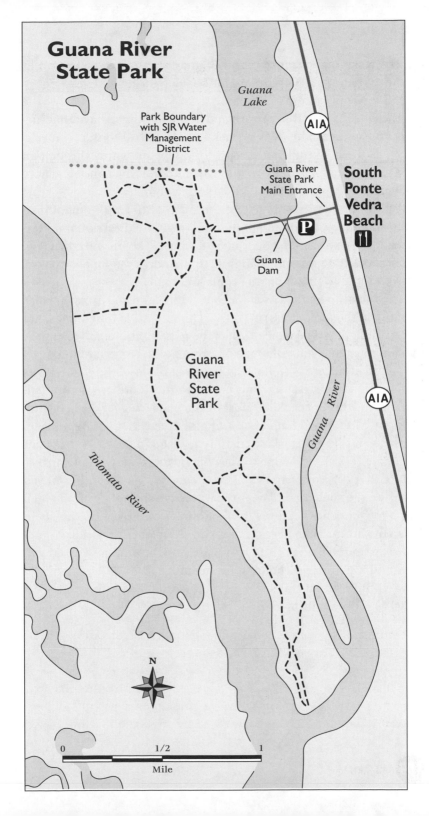

Guana River State Park

Guana
Lake

Park Boundary
with SJR Water
Management
District

AIA

Guana River
State Park
Main Entrance

**South
Ponte
Vedra
Beach**

P

Guana
Dam

Guana
River
State
Park

Guana River

Tolomato River

AIA

N

0   1/2   1
Mile

trances. Take the entrance to the Guana Dam use area. The other entrances (north and south) are for beach parking and offer no access to the trail system.

The ride starts at the western end of the parking area at the Guana Dam use area. The double-track entrance road to the dam continues as the bike trail to the west for a few 100 yards through an open grassy field. From there it moves into the tree canopy, where you'll find a sign-in book and kiosk with trail maps.

The trails (mostly double track) branch off from the main road at the sign-in area and are not marked with any directional preferences. Pick the direction you want to go and make up your own trip. To the south the trails circle around; to the north they meet up with the water management district trails and roads.

The trails are marked by color code with cut-in chevrons on poles pointing in the direction(s) of travel. The colors are trail names, not level of difficulty. The total length of the park trails is about 8.5 miles, though you could squeeze out a few more with some circling.

The road surface is well packed in most places; it has a few roots but is otherwise as fast or slow as you want. There are no difficult sections or hills to speak of. Most of the trails pass under a beautiful mature hardwood hammock and pine tree canopy. The trails on the western side of the island (mainly marked in red) suffered a fair amount of tree blowdown in the last hurricane, and the trail narrows a bit with a carryover or two. This area also has a number of red cedars on the shell mound near the water. On the Yellow Trail you'll find a few benches scattered around and a covered viewing stand over a freshwater marsh. Fast riders can complete these trails in well under an hour even with a few stops. Most will want to set aside an hour and a half to two hours for a leisurely ride with a chance to view wildlife (the usual suspects, with some feral hogs and occasional black bears thrown in).

3　Highlands Hammock State Park

There are some pretty rides in this popular family park, but they're not very long and some are too sandy. The ride on the paved entrance road passes through some of the finest virgin wetland hardwood hammock in the world. It's spectacular! This is my favorite single visual area in any park in the state. The unpaved trails are relatively good, except those that allow horses. The animals break through the top surface of the trails, which makes for very uncomfortable and difficult bicycle riding.

Activities:

Location: Highlands County

Trails: Paved road, 3.0 miles; dirt double track, 8.5 miles

Food: There is a park store and concession off the park entrance road.

Lodging and Camping: There are 138 full-hookup campsites available in the park. You'll find motels on US 27 in Sebring or Avon Park.

Contact: Highlands Hammock State Park, 5931 Hammock Road, Sebring, FL 33872; (941) 386–6094.

* *

The land for Highlands Hammock State Park was purchased in 1931. This was one of the four original Florida parks created in 1935 by the federal Civilian Conservation Corps. Each of its trails is different. The entrance road is paved and runs through the hardwood hammock to various points of interest. You can leave your car by the entrance station and ride to all parts of the park, including some incredibly beautiful virgin hardwood wetland systems.

A small cut-across on the western side also goes through hammock until it reaches the straight-line unpaved grassy trail along the northern border. This trail is on a raised roadbed through a swampy area. It's not as pretty as the paved park road but is a pleasure to ride when it's dry. The trail eventually runs into the administration buildings and circles around to a sandy road that in dry weather has a number of unridable places where the surface has been torn up by the horse traffic.

This unpaved trail is part of a circle that crosses the park road in two places. The part near the ranger station is very sandy; when it heads farther east into the pine uplands, the canopy gives it some protection. It comes out at the paved road at the park entrance.

The riding on these trails is mixed. Some places are fun, others are just too sandy to ride. All trails are flat with little difficulty if you can avoid the sand. Ask for a trail map when you drive in.

A well-manicured double track through the woods

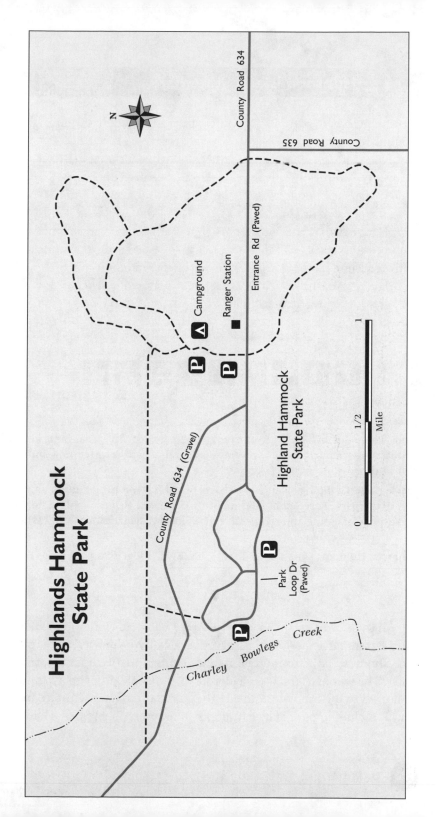

Highlands Hammock
State Park

County Road 634

County Road 635

N

Campground

Ranger Station

Entrance Rd (Paved)

County Road 634 (Gravel)

Highland Hammock
State Park

Park
Loop Dr
(Paved)

Charley Bowlegs Creek

0   1/2   1
              Mile

Hontoon Island State Park is an island in the middle of the St. Johns River, Florida's longest and most traveled river. The river starts in the marshes east of Melbourne to the south and flows north until it enters the Atlantic Ocean at Jacksonville. The river has been an important travel and recreational resource since William Bartram's travels in the 1700s, as it was for Native Americans long before that. With clear springs, large black-water lakes, wildlife refuges, and state parks, the St. Johns River system has something for everyone. Hontoon Island State Park is west of the city of Deland, about a third of the way from the river's source. It's accessible only by park ferry or private boat.

Activities:

Location: Volusia County

Trails: Dirt double track, 6.0 miles

Food: There is a small store at the park headquarters with restaurants and marina stores across the river on the mainland, which is only a few hundred yards away.

Lodging and Camping: There are six rustic cabins and twelve tent campsites in the park. Forty-eight boat mooring docks are also available. There is additional camping and rooms for rent at local marinas along with luxurious houseboat rentals.

Contact: Hontoon Island State Park, 2309 River Ridge Road, Deland, FL 32720; (904) 736–5309.

• •

This park was established in 1967 on 1,650-acre Hontoon Island. Before its acquisition, it served as a Native American site, pioneer homestead, commercial fishing center, boatyard, and cattle ranch. The whole island is considered an archaeological site. No one is allowed to dig anywhere inside the park boundaries without approval, including park staff. Human habitation probably dates back

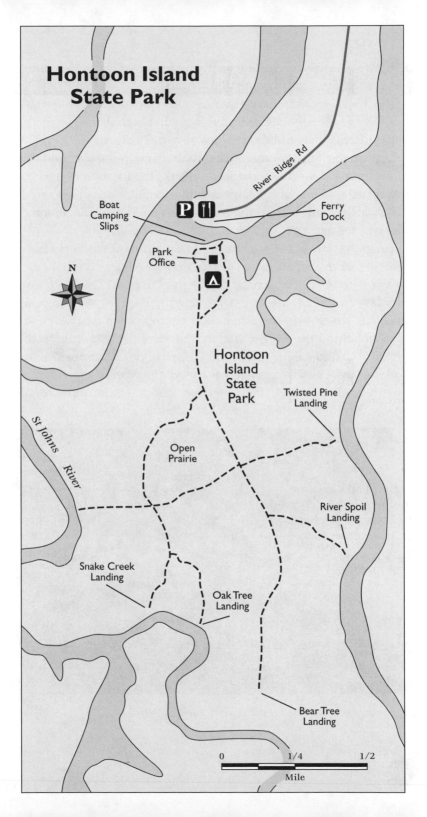

Hontoon Island State Park

River Ridge Rd

P **⊠**

Boat Camping Slips

Ferry Dock

Park Office ◼

⛺

N

Hontoon Island State Park

Twisted Pine Landing

St Johns River

Open Prairie

River Spoil Landing

Snake Creek Landing

Oak Tree Landing

Bear Tree Landing

0   1/4   1/2
Mile

more than 5,000 years. Ancient shell middens exist along the island's periphery at the ends of some of the trails.

The double-track trails at Hontoon are relatively short but make for a pleasant family ride. Mosquitoes will abound whenever the temperature is high and the breezes are low. Ticks should be plentiful in the warmer months. A one-night camp and ride would be fun for most folks. Blue Springs State Park, the location of a major clear spring and one of the largest winter populations of manatees in the state, is only a few miles to the east by river and about 25 miles by road.

The ride starts in the parking lot to the north of the park. Pedal about 50 feet to a small ferry (people and bicycles only) that takes you a few hundred feet across the river to the park. The ferry runs every few minutes and is free. However, there is the usual park entrance fee, payable on the other side. Then proceed east along the dirt road behind the ranger station and store for 0.25 mile to the campground and cabins. The road passes under a canopied hardwood–cabbage palm hammock that fringes the island and holds a lot of water after rains and when the river floods. Under most conditions, however, it maintains a ridable base.

The view from the ferry crossing the St. Johns River to the park

Riding the island trail

Past the campground the road heads through the higher open-center part of the island. Once cattle range, this area is reverting to pine-palmetto and wiregrass communities. You can take the fork to the left or right with about the same results. It's a nice trip through the uplands and down to the edge of the river at the margins.

The far southern end of the Timucuan Trail Road was under water when we were there, but otherwise the road was fine for riding. The nature trail—off limits to bikes—was also under water because of high-river conditions. We saw a lot of bear scat on the road and indications of deer and other animals. The trail map is easy to read, and the trails are quite predictable.

Jonathan Dickinson State Park is 11,500 acres of flatwoods scrubland east of Hobe Sound, containing hiking trails as well as Loxahatchee River access, camping, and concessions. The Loxahatchee is the only federally designated Wild and Scenic River in Florida. The river is on the western side of the park and available for boating and fishing activities. The Hobe Sound National Wildlife Refuge is just north and across U.S. 1 from the park.

Activities:

Location: Martin County

Trails: Paved park roads, 5.0 miles; paved nonmotorized bike path, 1.5 miles; dirt double tracks, 8.0 miles

Food: There are some snacks and other camp food at the store in the park on the banks of the Loxahatchee River, 5 miles from the entrance. Restaurants and food stores are located 5 miles north at Hobe Sound, or 7 miles south at Tequesta.

Lodging and Camping: The park has twelve cabins and 135 campsites, most with electricity and water. Motels and hotels are located at Hobe Sound and Tequesta.

Contact: Jonathan Dickinson State Park, 16450 Southeast Federal Highway, Hobe Sound, FL 33455; (561) 546-2771.

• •

This park was officially opened in 1950 after a short stint as an army base (Camp Murphy Signal Corps School) during World War II. It's an unusual refuge in the middle of a rapidly urbanizing part of the state. Though the land is generally flat, you'll find a diverse trail system and interesting camping along the river. The paved park entrance road is a nice flat 5-mile (one way) ride to the river and campgrounds. It travels though many of the park's coastal ecosystems, and has heavy traffic only on weekends and during special events.

The paved nonmotorized bike path is a pleasant but short ride on a closed-off old road with fair tree cover that will eventually make

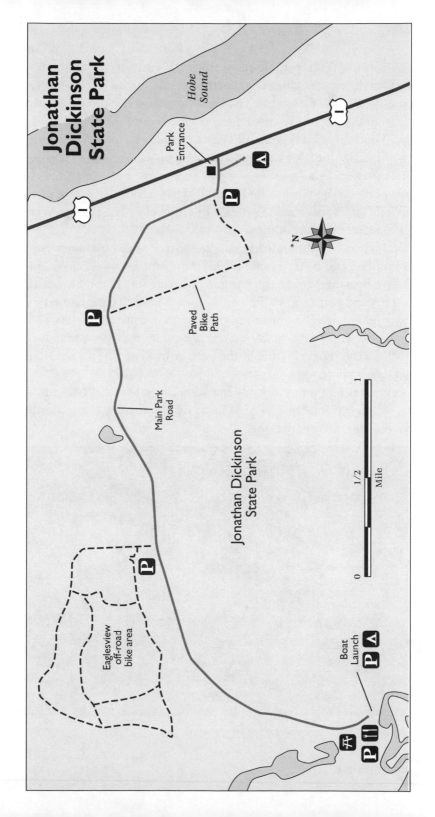

Jonathan Dickinson State Park

Hobe Sound

Park Entrance

Paved Bike Path

Main Park Road

Jonathan Dickinson State Park

Eaglesview off-road bike area

Boat Launch

N

0   1/2   1
Mile

a nice canopy. This path starts at the park entrance road about a mile from the ranger station next to the active railroad tracks. It travels next to the line for a while and then turns east back to the southern part of the paved park road. Because there is no motorized traffic allowed and the road is generally flat and wide, it's a good easy ride for families, including kids with training wheels.

The unpaved trail system starts at Eagleview, on your right just as you come to the power-line crossing of the park road. There is an open field and horse watering trough but little else. The signs to your right indicate the start of the trails.

Under good conditions (dry, but not too dry, with little horse use) these trails could be enjoyable to ride. Unfortunately, service vehicles have broken through the hardpan, causing lots of mud holes after a rain and soft sand in the open areas. The trails are named by color, which can be confusing to those who are used to colors designating difficulty. The markings are decent if you have a map (obtainable at the ranger station at the park entrance), but it's not hard to get lost if you don't.

At press time there was some question about the quality of these trails for bike riders, but there is hope for the future, given a little TLC, and some reengineering.

The paved non-motorized trail is great for the whole family

Maclay State Gardens is a large park between urban Tallahassee and suburban Leon County. It has marvelous formal gardens, two lakes, and a series of trails, all on former plantation
lands at the foot of the Red Hills district. The district consists
of a large group of old, mainly cotton, plantations that occupy
the northern part of Leon County into southern Georgia. Most
were used as hunting lodges after the mid-1800s. The old fields
have regrown naturally into an upland magnolia hardwood-pine
forest; this covers most of the property that isn't part of the plantation house gardens. The manor house in the garden area, open
to public viewing, retains its old furnishings, and the outbuild-
ings are presently used for conferences and weddings. The
paved trail goes through some of the garden area, and the unpaved trails are all under the forest canopy of the regrown fields.
In addition to the riding trails, there are hiking-only trails in
both park and gardens; horses are available for rent on most
weekends. The horses use the double-track dirt trails.

Activities:

Location: Leon County

Trails: Paved roads, 1.5 miles; dirt double track, 5.0 miles; dirt single track, 3.0 miles

Food: Vending machines are available at the park buildings. All the food and fuel you could want is found starting a few hundred yards south of the entrance of Maclay Gardens, around the intersection of US 319 and I-10.

Lodging and Camping: Motels are available along US 319 and I-10

Contact: Maclay State Gardens, 3540 Thomasville Road, Tallahassee, FL 32308; (850) 487-4556.

• • • • • • • • • • • • • • • • • • • •

The garden portion of this park is the former estate of Alfred B.
Maclay, a New York financier who bought the property in 1922.
His widow donated it to the state in 1953. In 1994 Florida acquired

the adjacent Overstreet Addition to the west (877 acres), where you'll find a pristine lake and unpaved trails around it.

The trails at Maclay can be accessed either from the Forest Meadows side on the west or the formal park entrance from Thomasville Road on the east. There are three types of trails in the park; paved, dirt double track, and dirt single track. The paved park entrance road goes through mature virgin hardwoods and passes the cutoff to the Lake Hall swimming and boating area as well as garden entrances to end up at the parking area for the off-road trails. It has a few more hills than most Florida trails, but it's a nice family ride unless the traffic gets heavy during special events.

The older unpaved trails are relatively smooth double tracks used by maintenance vehicles, horses, runners, walkers, birders, and bikers. These are dirt and clay with some mud thrown in after rains. They can be ridden at high speeds on weekdays, and with care on busier weekends. All the trails in the park are canopied with upland hardwoods that have grown back in what were plantation fields many years ago.

The Lake Trail is a circular loop around Lake Overstreet that starts at the end of the paved park road. It's about 3 miles long and contains a few nice climbs up red clay hills with fast downhills on the other side. You can see Lake Overstreet from many places on the trail (particularly in the winter when the leaves have fallen), and there is one short cutoff directly to the lake, where you'll find a covered picnic and pit toilet area. A few old tenant farmer houses along

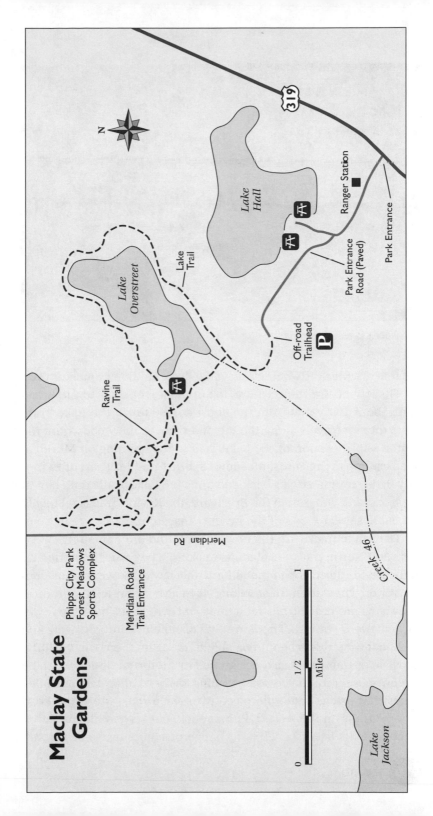

Horse riders on the Ravine Trail

the trail are presently being excavated; look but don't touch or take.

The Ravine Trail starts at the top of a steep hill, called the Brickyard, about 100 yards from the short connector to the Lake Trail. From there it travels along the top of a ridge in the woods from the southwestern portion of the Lake Trail to the crossing on Meridian Road leading to the Forest Meadows Sports Complex (part of Phipps City Park). It then circles back and joins the Lake Trail connector at the Brickyard. Other than the Brickyard, the Ravine Trail is relatively flat but has great views of the ravine ecosystem.

The single tracks are the newest trails and are named the West, East, and North Trails for obvious reasons. They run from one end of the Ravine Trail loop to the other with a few crossovers of the double tracks. They are easiest to find at the Meridian Road entrance. They twist around and between trees and over roots, but they're not particularly technical. There are few or no elevation changes, and even first-time riders should be able to navigate them successfully.

None of the trails has a designated or preferred direction, so be careful of users coming at you. Funding has been allocated for a bike-pedestrian bridge (or underpass) over (or under) Meridian Road from the trails on the west in Phipps Park, but start and completion dates have not been set. This is a dangerous crossing, so be careful.

Manatee Springs State Park is located 6 miles west of Chiefland on more than 2,000 acres of woodlands, adjacent to a crystal-clear first-magnitude spring that flows a short distance to the Suwannee River. The paved entrance road is a pleasant 2-mile ride, even with the occasional vehicles. The off-road trails are all double tracks under a tree canopy in hardwood hammock and sandhill communities. These are easy, fun trails for the whole family. Most good riders can travel all the trails in the park in less than an hour. Even slower riders will like these trails for general playing around and wildlife viewing at the right times of day. The mouth of the Suwannee River is only 23 miles from the park, creating great opportunities for boating and fishing as well as scuba diving in the spring itself.

Activities:

Location: Levy County

Trails: Paved road, 2.0 miles; dirt double track, 8.5 miles

Food: The concessions area near the main spring has snacks. Restaurants and food stores are located in Chiefland, 6 miles to the east.

Lodging and Camping: There are a hundred campsites in the park, most with electricity and water. Motels are in Chiefland.

Contact: Manatee Springs State Park, 11650 Northwest 115th Street, Chiefland, FL 32626; (352) 493–6072.

• • • • • • • • • • • • • • • • • • • •

M anatee Springs became a park in 1955. It's an early habitation site of the Weedon Indians and other Native Americans dating back many thousands of years. The explorer William Bartram visited the spring in 1774 and described it in his writings.

Manatee Springs State Park's paved entrance road is the usual asphalt blacktop, and it winds from the entrance station to the spring and campground areas. The 2-mile ride should tempt anyone with a bike handy, even if you only came to swim or canoe.

The unpaved trails are dirt double tracks without the usual problems caused by horses. The trails mostly travel under forest canopy through mature river hardwood hammock with some big pines thrown in on the sandhills. There are some pretty little black-water ponds in the northeastern corner of the double-track area (Shacklefoot Trail) surrounded by large cypress trees—a glimpse of old Florida. The trails are mostly flat, and though the surface is a little soft in spots, it's generally hard-packed sand with lots of grassy areas.

When the Suwannee River is in flood, some of these trails will be blocked by water. Rainy weather may cause problems with muddy areas. The trails are all marked by signs at the intersections. These include locator maps indicating exactly where you are. There are still intersections that are not marked, and the dead end signs really mean "dead end." They don't go anywhere, but could be connected to points of interest in the future with some work. Get trail maps at the ranger station when you come in.

The map locator system

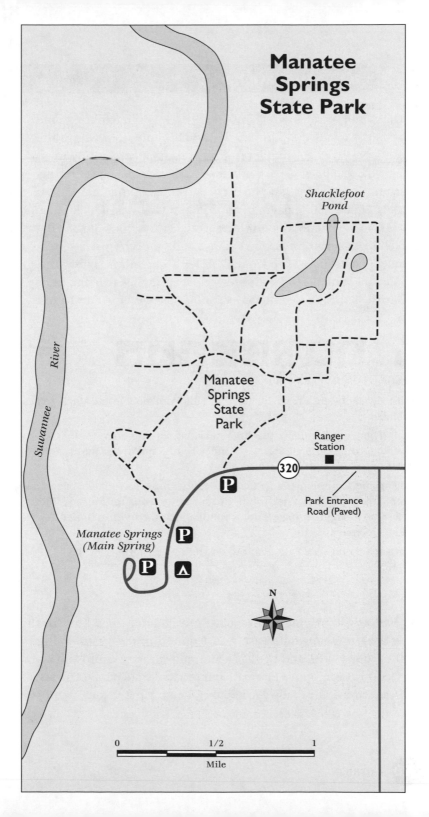

Manatee Springs State Park

Shacklefoot Pond

Manatee
Springs
State
Park

Suwannee River

Ranger Station

320

Park Entrance Road (Paved)

P

P

Manatee Springs (Main Spring)

P

N

0   1/2   1
Mile

The major feature of O'Leno State Park is the Santa Fe land bridge, a hardwood hammock and sinkhole area where the Santa Fe River goes underground and reappears a mile or so later. The 6,000-acre park provides places for horseback riding, swimming, fishing, and boating as well as biking and nature trails. It has a large pavilion and kitchen facilities, which make it a favorite destination for folks from Gainesville who use the buildings and grounds for weddings and fraternity parties. Itchetucknee Springs State Park, 12 miles away, offers swimming, canoeing, tubing, and rafting on a clear spring-fed run that feeds into the Santa Fe River near its confluence with the Suwannee.

Activities:

Location: Alachua and Columbia Counties

Trails: Paved entrance road, 2.0 miles; dirt and sand double and single tracks, 13.0 miles

Food: There's a soft drink machine near the parking area. Food and supplies are located in High Springs, 7 miles south, and at the intersection of US 441 and I–75, 5 miles north.

Lodging and Camping: There are sixty-four campsites with electricity and water in the park; seventeen cabins are currently being refurbished. Motels are located in High Springs, 7 miles south and at the intersection of US 441 and I–75, 5 miles north.

Contact: O'Leno State Park, Route 2, Box 1010, High Springs, FL 32643; (904) 454–1853.

• •

P art of the original Pensacola–St. Augustine road built in the 1820s, O'Leno State Park was acquired in the 1930s and used by the federal WPA and CCC as a summer forestry camp and training facility. It was one of Florida's four original state parks. The state's earliest cross-state roadway, Bellamy Road, runs through and is a

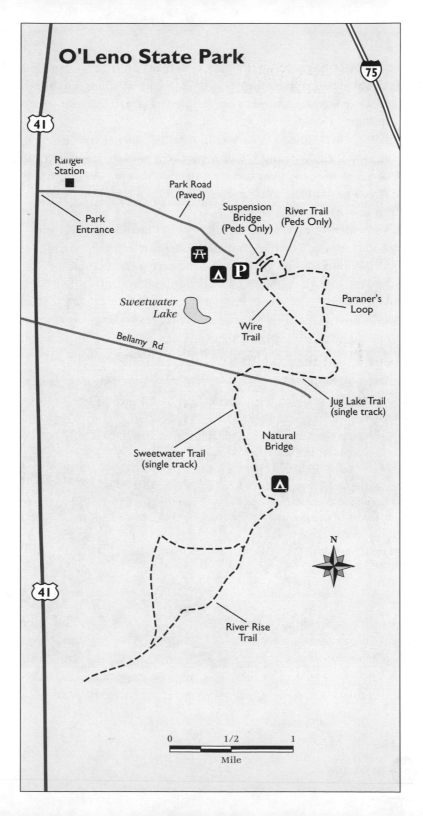

O'Leno State Park

75

41

Ranger
Station

Park Road
(Paved)

Park
Entrance

Suspension
Bridge
(Peds Only)

River Trail
(Peds Only)

P

Paraner's
Loop

*Sweetwater
Lake*

Bellamy Rd

Wire
Trail

Jug Lake Trail
(single track)

Natural
Bridge

Sweetwater Trail
(single track)

41

N

River Rise
Trail

0   1/2   1

Mile

part of some of the trails in the park. There are interpretative signs along the road describing how it was built, the excavations conducted by the archaeologists, and what has happened to it in the years since construction.

Finding the trailhead is very confusing because it isn't marked, and the bike trail starts next to or is part of a pedestrians-only trail. Both have their origins near the suspension bridge by the swimming area. If you park in the main parking lot and go east, you'll eventually run into a trail you can ride.

If you can't find the trail near the bridge, head south and something will show up. The park trail map is a little difficult to read, but is very helpful once you get to know the area a bit. It shows all the trails and indicates a double track with a solid line, and a single track by a dotted line.

The Wire Trail is the trail easiest to find from the campground. It's a double track with some long sandy places that are unridable if used recently by horses. The rest of the trail is a hard dirt surface

Parener's Loop double-track trail

within the tree canopy. The Wire Trail is met by a single track at its connection with Parener's Loop.

The first part of the single track (1.5 miles) is a little twisty, with a mostly smooth sandy surface and a few roots. It passes Jug Lake, a small sinkhole next to the trail, on its way to Bellamy Road.

The second single track that goes from Bellamy Road to Sweetwater is rooty and rough as you'll find anywhere. It's mostly within the upper floodplain and will be impassable when the river is high. There are no real hills or technical sections—other than the roots, which aren't difficult to ride but bounce the heck out of you for most of the way.

When you come back from Sweetwater, you can pick up Parener's Loop to the east. It's a nice smooth double track that passes small but interesting sinkhole lakes; it has fewer sandy places than the Wire Trail.

You should be able to ride all 13 miles of trails in less than two hours if you pedal continuously. Look for wildlife at the usual times. We almost ran over a fox on one trail and deer on another.

9   Oleta River State Recreation Area

The Oleta River State Recreation Area is the premier mountain bike trail facility in Florida's state park system. Located on 1,043 acres of mostly dredged spoil between the Oleta River, Intracoastal Waterway, and Biscayne Bay, it's the largest urban state park in Florida.

Activities:

Location: Dade County

Trails: Paved bike trail, 1.5 miles (parallels park entrance road); dirt single-track and limerock roads, 12–14 miles

Food: Just outside the park entrance, there are a number of commercial establishments in strip shopping centers on the northern side of State Road 826.

Lodging and Camping: There are fourteen primitive cabins (air-conditioning but no water or baths) in the recreation area. Motels and hotels are found 4 miles to the west at the interchange of I–95 and State Road 826, and a similar distance to the east in Miami Beach.

Contact: Oleta River SRA, 3400 Northeast 163rd Street, North Miami, FL 33160; (305) 919–1846.

• •

The banks of the Oleta River have been occupied for the last 2,500 years by Native Americans, who were displaced in colonial times by early Florida settlers using the river as an access from Biscayne Bay into the Everglades. The banks of the river were farmed for pineapples and vegetables in the late 1800s. This state recreation area became part of the state park system in the late 1970s.

Though surrounded by a reestablished mangrove fringe, the greater part of this park is composed of Australian pine and other exotic plants (efforts are under way to replace many of these with native vegetation). The land contours outside the high-public-use areas are fairly rough, giving more relief than you expect on off-road trails in southern Florida.

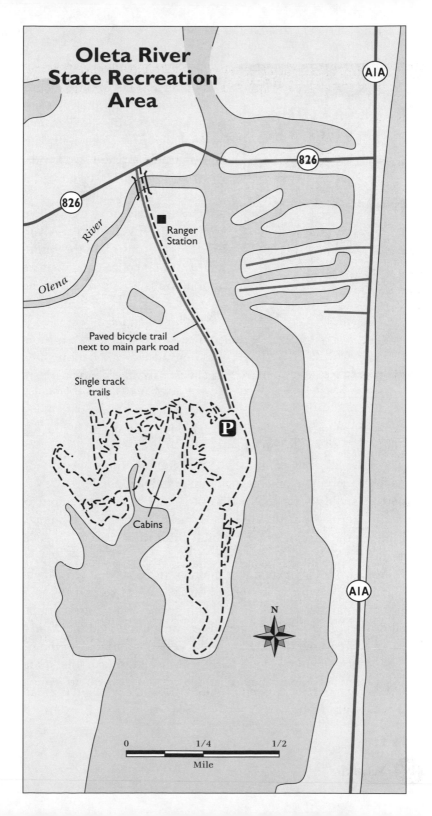

NEARBY RECREATIONAL AMENITIES

You'll find great swimming, fishing, and sunbathing on the shores of Biscayne Bay inside the park, as well as numerous areas of interest in the surrounding communities. Check out John U. Lloyd Beach SRA, John Pennekamp Coral Reef State Park, Bill Baggs Cape Florida SRA, Hugh Taylor Birch SRA, and Biscayne Bay and Everglades National Parks.

The park includes beaches, rustic cabins and covered pavilions available for rent, a fishing pier, rest room facilities with showers, and paved and unpaved bike trails. This is a popular park on weekends, with more than 60,000 bikers a year riding the off-road trails.

This park is a great example of community involvement: A volunteer bike patrol helps build, maintain, and police the trails. The off-road trails are used during the year for local, state, and national mountain bike races.

The paved trail goes from the park entrance to the parking area and beaches alongside the park entrance road. It's an 8-foot-wide asphalt byway along the level portions of the park. This trail is suitable for skaters and bikers, including those with training wheels.

The off-road trails combine the flat gravelly limerock service roads with rooty, twisty, and rocky up-and-down single tracks developed specifically for mountain bikes. The trails are marked as novice or intermediate. All of the single track is inside the tree canopy, and though the surface can get muddy after rains, it stays in good shape during dry periods.

The novice trails include the limerock roads as well as some of the single tracks which are twisty but have fewer roots and rocks than these marked intermediate. Though the single tracks are labeled novice, they probably should be considered beginner trails, since some first-time riders may not be very comfortable on them.

The intermediate trails are fairly technical and take lots of energy and concentration. They meander up and down 6- to 15-foot

An urban park with great trails shows off at the Florida State Mountain Bike championshops

mounds of dirt and limerock. Some of the twists in the trails are more than 90 degrees and often include roots or drops. The roots can be large with a few log jumps that are mainly buttressed and can be ridden without chainringing. The approaches to the mounds are often pretty steep, with tight turns at the tops. The downs off the mounds can be quite sharp; roots add an extra challenge. There are no long climbs or high hills, but rocks and roots are everywhere on the intermediate trails, often with only a few inches of clearance. Some of these trails would be better marked intermediate/advanced.

This park is located a few miles south of Sarasota on US 41. Sarasota Gulf beaches are nearby, with all their amenities. The park preserves pinewoods scrubland, which is fast disappearing in Florida. A needed home to the threatened scrub jay and other animals and plants that inhabit this almost desertlike sandy system, it also contains areas of wet hammock and upland pine-palmetto habitat that are in close proximity to the camping areas. The trail system was developed on park service roads with the same kinds of problems and benefits found in other parks.

Activities: 🏕️ 🚲 🚴 🚶 🦌

Location: Sarasota County

Trails: Paved park road, 2.0 miles; unpaved double track, 15.4 miles

Food: Available on US 41 north and south of the park entrance.

Lodging and Camping: There are 104 campsites in the park, almost all with electricity and water. Motels are located on US 41 a short distance from the park entrance.

Contact: Florida Park Service, 1843 South Tamiami Trail, Osprey, FL 34229; (941) 483–5956.

• •

This park opened in 1956 on 462 acres of land donated in the memory of Oscar Scherer by his daughter. An additional 922 acres was acquired in 1991, for a total of 1,384 acres.

The 2-mile park entrance road is paved and available for riding. The off-road unpaved trails are often open, sandy double tracks with some grass. There are a few canopied areas on the White Trail, but the rest is open to the sky. The trails are also used by service vehicles but no horses. Because of the sandy conditions during dry periods, you can expect some difficulties unless you have the strength to motor through the soft patches. The Friends of Oscar Scherer Park provides a map of all the trails.

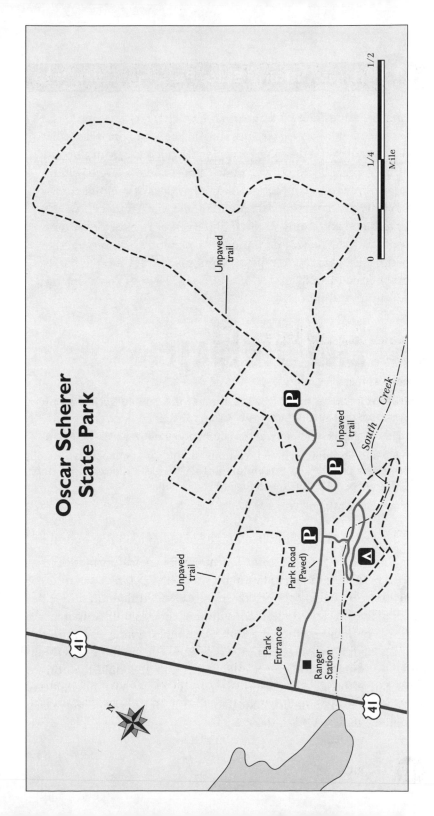

Oscar Scherer State Park

Unpaved trail

Unpaved trail

Unpaved trail

41

41

Park Entrance

Park Road (Paved)

Ranger Station

South Creek

P

P

P

N

0   1/4   1/2

Mile

Paynes Prairie State Preserve is more than 20,000 acres of prairie (or lake, depending on circumstances) just south of Gainesville. Because of its fluctuating water levels and the reintroduction of bison and wild horses, the prairie has become a prime wildlife viewing area. One of Florida's resident flocks of sandhill cranes (and large winter migratory populations) stays here, as do some introduced whooping cranes. The preserve also enjoys large populations of ducks and reptiles. We wouldn't recommend this park just for biking, but when combined with other activities in the area it could make for a pleasant late-fall, early-spring, or winter outing.

Activities:

Location: Alachua County

Trails: Paved park entrance road, 2.6 miles; dirt double track, 18.0 miles (small number of single-track connectors)

Food: Available in Micanopy to the south, and 6 miles north on US 441.

Lodging and Camping: There is camping in the park (Wauberg Lake facility) on thirty-five RV and fifteen tent sites. There is a motel at exit 73 on I–75, and more on US 441 north toward Gainesville.

Contact: Paynes Prairie Preserve, Route 2, Box 41, Micanopy, FL 32677–9702.

• •

This 21,000-acre preserve is a major geological formation that has seen human habitation for the last 10,000-plus years. Over the course of geological periods the area would flood and dry, depending on the capacity and condition of the Alachua Sink near its northern boundary. When the sink was open, the area was a prairie; when closed, it was a lake. In the late 1800s the sinkhole was dynamited by ranchers to keep it open so that cattle could feed on its grass. Since the state acquired the park in the 1980s, the sink has been left to its own devices. Mother Nature once more determines its status.

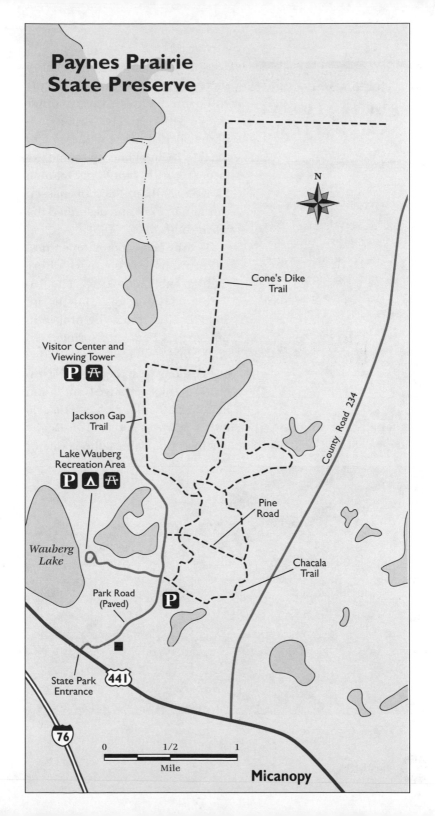

Paynes Prairie
State Preserve

N

Cone's Dike
Trail

Visitor Center and
Viewing Tower
P **⛺**

Jackson Gap
Trail

Lake Wauberg
Recreation Area
P **△** **⛺**

*Wauberg
Lake*

County Road 234

Pine
Road

Chacala
Trail

Park Road
(Paved)
P

State Park
Entrance

441

76

0   1/2   1
Mile

Micanopy

You'll find great swimming, fishing, and sunbathing on the shores of Biscayne Bay inside the park, as well as numerous areas of interest in the surrounding communities. Check out John U. Lloyd Beach SRA, John Pennekamp Coral Reef State Park, Bill Baggs Cape Florida SRA, Hugh Taylor Birch SRA, and Biscayne Bay and Everglades National Parks.

Human habitation probably started with the mammoth hunters and continued with various other Native American civilizations until the Spanish came to the area in the late 1600s, when it became the largest cattle ranch in Spanish Florida. William Bartram passed through in 1774 and described the basin in his diary.

Nearby Recreational Amenities: Lake Wauberg in the park offers fishing and picnicking. The 15-mile-long Gainesville-Hawthorne State Trail is across the prairie to the north at Boulware Springs (see Trail 7 in the rail-trail section of this book), along with the park's Northern Rim Interpretative Center and its foot-traffic-only trails. Historic Micanopy is a few miles to the south and worth a visit. The Devils Millhopper State Geological Site northwest of Gainesville is one of

The very sandy Cone's Dike Trail

Horses move over to let bike riders pass on Chacala Trail

the state's more spectacular sinkholes, with nice walking trails. San Felasco Hammock State Preserve northwest of Gainesville also has good hiking in mature climax mesic hammock.

The park's paved entrance road is a nice ride under big trees. It's used by skaters and cars but still a pleasant family trip.

The unpaved trails are of mixed value. Where the trail is used by service vehicles and horses along with bikes and there is no tree canopy (on Cone's Dike Trail, for example), there are some very sandy and rough places. These are often unridable, and you need to be prepared to walk your bike.

The trails that are mostly inside the hammock canopy can be good or bad depending on horse traffic and recent rain. A few of the connector trails are single tracks, but for the most part the unpaved trails are old ranch roads used by the park for service vehicles. There are no technical trails, but the places where horses haven't broken through the surface are fast and fun to ride. Make sure you get a trail map at the entrance; this describes each of the trails.

The Office of Greenways & Trails

The Office of Greenways & Trails (OGT), within the Florida Department of Environmetal Protection, serves as a focal point for the growing greenways and trails system in Florida. The office provides a range of services from assisting communities with local projects to providing Florida's residents and visitors with information regarding recreational opportunities on greenways and trails.

OGT's primary task is overseeing implementation of Florida's vision for a connected statewide system of greenways and trails. This vision is outlined in a five-year plan titled Connecting Florida's Communities. An underlying goal of this plan is that every Floridian should be able to leave his or her house andl within minutes, be traveling along a natural corridor that connects to a park, conservation area or city center. A grand ambition indeed. But one that offers Florida a comprehensive way of integrating conervation and recreation, and connecting Florida's communities.

The Florida Greenways and Trails System has its roots in the Florida Recreational Trails System, the Florida Canoe Trail System, and the public parks, forests, refuges, wildlife management areas and water management areas created to protect Florida's natural heritage.

Created by the Legislature in 1979, the recreational trails system provides people with access to and enjoyment of outdoor recration areas, and provides an essential framework for the recreational elements of today's greenways and trails system.

The vision of a system of greenways crisscrossing the state, connecting communities and conservation areas, began taking root in Florida nearly a decade ago. What began as a project undertaken by 1000 Friends of Florida and the Conservation Fund in 1991 quickly became a statewide initiative with the creation by Governor Chiles in 1993 of the Florida Greenways Commission. That public-private group made a bold recommendation: Florida should create a statewide system of greenways, a system that would link natrual areas and open spaces, conserviing native landscapes and ecosystems and offering recreational opportunities across the state. This "green infrastructure" would connect residents and visitors to the state's natural and cultural heritage, enhance their sense of place, and enrich their quality of life.

The Governor and Legislature agreed, and in 1995 appointed the Florida Greenways Coordingating Council (FGCC) to continue the sommission's work. They also directed the Florida Department of Environmental Protection (FDEP0 to take the lead in the state's greenways efforts. Parallel to this, the Florida Recreational Trails Council (FRTC) continued to review the proposed network of recreational trails in the context of a statewide-connected system. Ultimatlely recognizing the importance of integrating the connected ecological and recreational systems, the Legislature created the Florida Greenways & Trails Council in 1999 to collectively replace the Fgcc and FRTC. Today, that council, staffed by the Fdep Office of Greenways & Trails, serves as a voice for Florida's connected system of ecological and recreational corridors.

Currently, the office of Greenways & Trails is spending much of its resources on the "super-connectors" in the statewide system: the marjorie harris Carr Cross Florida Greenway, located in central Florida along the corridor of the former Cross FLorida Barge Canal (managed by OGT); the Lake Okeechobee Scenic Trail, a muli-use trail which encircles the second larges freshwater lake in the United States; and the Florida Keys Overseas Heritage Trail, an ambitious project which will reconnect the bridges of the historic Overseas Railroad. All of these are described in detail in this guide.

For further information about the Office of Greenways & Trails or these projects, call toll free 1–877–822–5208.

VISIT FLORIDA™

Financial assistance for this guide given by the Florida
Tourism Industry Marketing Corporation (www.flausa.com).

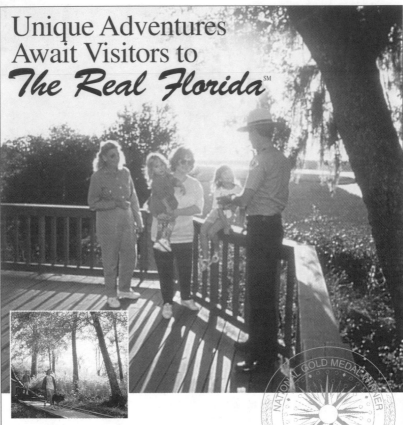

Florida's Award-winning State Parks

Alafia River S.R.A.
Alfred B. Maclay S.G./Lake
   Overstreet Trail
Amelia Island S.R.A.
Anastasia S.R.A.
Anclote Key S.PR.
Bahia Honda S.P.
Big Lagoon S.R.A.
Big Talbot Island S.P.
Bill Baggs Cape Florida S.R.A.
Blackwater Heritage S.T.
Blackwater River S.P.
Blue Spring S.P.
Bulow Creek S.P.
Bulow Plantation Ruins S.H.S.
Caladesi Island S.P.
Cayo Costa S.P.
Cedar Key S.M.
Cedar Key Scrub S.R.
Collier-Seminole S.P.
Constitution Convention S.M.
Crystal River S.A.S.
Dade Battlefield S.H.S.
Dead Lakes S.R.A.
DeLeon Springs S.R.A.
Delnor-Wiggins Pass S.R.A.
Devil's Millhopper S.G.S.
Don Pedro Island S.R.A.
Econfina River S.P.
Eden S.G.
Egmont Key S.P.
Fakahatchee Strand S.PR.
Falling Waters S.R.A.
Fanning Springs S.R.A.
Faver-Dykes S.P.
Florida Caverns S.P.
Forest Capital S.M.
Fort Clinch S.P.
Fort Cooper S.P.
Fort George Island S.C.S.
Fort Pierce Inlet S.R.A./
   Avalon S.R.A.
Fort Zachary Taylor S.H.S.
Gainesville to Hawthorne S.T.

Gamble Plantation S.H.S.
Gamble Rogers Mem. S.R.A. at
   Flagler Beach
Gasparilla Island S.R.A.
Grayton Beach S.R.A.
Guana River S.P.
Henderson Beach S.R.A.
Highlands Hammock S.P.
Hillsborough River S.P.
Homosassa Springs S.W.P.
Honeymoon Island S.R.A.
Hontoon Island S.P.
Hugh Taylor Birch S.R.A.
Ichetucknee Springs S.P.
Indian Key S.H.S.
John D. MacArthur Beach S.P.
John Gorrie S.M.
John Pennekamp Coral Reef S.P.
John U. Lloyd Beach S.R.A.
Jonathan Dickinson S.P.
Key Largo Hammocks S.B.S.
Kissimmee Prairie S.PR.
Koreshan S.H.S.
Lake Griffin S.R.A.
Lake Jackson Mounds S.A.S.
Lake Kissimmee S.P.
Lake Louisa S.P.
Lake Manatee S.R.A.
Lignumvitae Key S.B.S.
Little Manatee River S.P.
Little Talbot Island S.P.
Long Key S.R.A.
Lovers Key S.R.A.
Lower Wekiva River S.PR.
Manatee Springs S.P.
Marjorie Kinnan Rawlings S.H.S.
Mike Roess Gold Head Branch S.P.
Myakka River S.P.
Natural Bridge Battlefield S.H.S.
O'Leno S.P./River Rise S.P.
Ochlockonee River S.P.
Oleta River S.R.A.
Olustee Battlefield S.H.S.
Oscar Scherer S.P.

Paynes Creek S.H.S.
Paynes Prairie S.PR.
Peacock Springs S.R.A.
Perdido Key S.R.A.
Ponce De Leon Springs S.R.A.
Rainbow Springs S.P.
Ravine S.G.
River Bluff Picnic Site
Rock Springs Run S.R.
Rocky Bayou S.R.A.
San Felasco Hammock S.PR.
San Marcos De Apalache S.H.S.
San Pedro Underwater A.P.
Savannas S.PR.
Sebastian Inlet S.R.A.
   (McLarty Treasure Museum)
Silver River S.P.
Skyway State Fishing Pier
St. Andrews S.R.A.
St. George Island S.P.
St. Joseph Péninsula S.P.
St. Lucie Inlet S.PR./
   Seabranch S.PR.
Stephen Foster State Folk
   Culture Center
Suwannee River S.P.
Tallahassee-St. Marks Historic
   Railroad S.T.
The Barnacle S.H.S.
Three Rivers S.R.A.
Tomoka S.P.
Topsail Hill S.PR.
Topsail Hill S.PR./Gregory E.
   Moore RV Resort Park
Torreya S.P.
Tosohatchee S.R.
Van Fleet, General James A. S.T.
Waccasassa Bay S.PR.
Wakulla Springs S.P. & Lodge
Washington Oaks S.G.
Wekiwa Springs S.P.
Windley Key Fossil Reef S.G.S.
Withlacoochee S.T.
Ybor City S.M.
Yulee Sugar Mill Ruins S.H.S.

The Real Florida^{SM}

For a free brochure, call 850-488-9872.
Internet: www.dep.state.fl.us/parks

FREE T!*

*with a $50 contribution or more

100% cotton T-shirt with Rails-to-Trails Conservancy logo printed on the front; and a circle of trail users printed in royal blue on back.

JOIN RAILS-TO-TRAILS CONSERVANCY NOW, get a FREE T-SHIRT and connect yourself with the largest national trail-building organization. As a member of Rails-to-Trails Conservancy, you will receive the following benefits:

- *Rails to Trails*, a colorful magazine dedicated to celebrating trails and greenways, published four times a year
- A free copy of *Sampler of America's Rail-Trails*
- Discounts on publications, merchandise and conferences
- A free t-shirt with your contribution of $50 or more
- Additional membership benefits for Trailblazer Society members, including invitation to the annual rail-trail excursions

Most importantly, you will have the satisfaction that comes from helping to build a nationwide network of beautiful trails for all of us to enjoy for years and generations to come.

PLEASE JOIN TODAY by calling toll-free: 1-800-888-7747, ext. 11 (credit card orders only), or mail your membership contribution with the form on the following page, or see our web site, **www.railtrails.org**.

RAILS-TO-TRAILS CONSERVANCY • *Connecting People and Communities*

Yes! I want to join Rails-to-Trails Conservancy!

Send me my member packet, including my *Sampler of America's Rail-Trails*, one year (four issues) of *Rails to Trails*, the colorful magazine that celebrates trails and greenways and my FREE T-SHIRT with my contribution of $50 or more. I will also receive discounts on publications, merchandise and conferences. Here is my membership gift of:

❑ $18 – Individual
❑ $25 – Supporting
❑ $50 – Patron *(Free t-shirt at this giving level or higher!)*

T-shirt size XL only

❑ $100 – Benefactor
❑ $500 – Advocate
❑ $1,000 – Trailblazer Society
❑ Other $_____

❑ Monthly Giving, *please see box below*

PAYMENT METHOD: ❑ VISA   ❑ MasterCard   ❑ American Express
Card # _____ Exp. Date _____
Signature _____
Member Name_____
Street _____
City _____ State _____ Zip _____
Telephone _____ email_____

Rails-to-Trails Conservancy is a non-profit charitable 501(c)(3) organization. Contributions are tax-deductible.

I want to support Rails-to-Trails Conservancy in the smartest, easiest and best way possible by donating monthly. Enclosed is my first monthly gift of:

❑ $5   ❑ $10   ❑ $15   ❑ Other $_____ *($5 minimum monthly contribution, please)*

Charge my future monthly gifts to my :
❑ Checking Account — Please transfer the amount indicated from my bank account each month
❑ Credit Card — Please charge the amount indicated to my credit card each month: ❑ VISA   ❑ MasterCard   ❑ American Express

Card Number: _____ Exp. Date: _____
Signature: _____ Date: _____

PAPERLESS PLEDGE AUTHORIZATION: I authorize Rails-to-Trails Conservancy to transfer my monthly contribution from my bank account or to charge my credit card (whichever I have indicated). I understand I may cancel or change my monthly pledge at any time by notifying Rails-to-Trails Conservancy. A record of each payment will appear on my monthly bank or credit card statement and will serve as my receipt.

Signature: _____ Date Signed: _____

EFT

Rails-to-Trails Conservancy
1100 17th St. NW • Washington, DC 20036
1-800-888-7747, ext. 11 (credit card orders only) • www.railtrails.org
To contact our membership department, please call (202) 974-5105 or email rtchelen@transact.org

RAILS to TRAILS CONSERVANCY

GUIDE